MARKETING
MOVES

MARKETING *MOVES*

A New Approach to Profits, Growth, and Renewal

PHILIP KOTLER
DIPAK C. JAIN
SUVIT MAESINCEE

HARVARD BUSINESS SCHOOL PRESS
BOSTON, MASSACHUSETTS

Library of Congress Cataloging-in-Publication Data

Kotler, Philip.
    Marketing moves : a new approach to profits, growth, and renewal /
Philip Kotler, Dipak C. Jain, Suvit Maesincee.
      p. cm.
    Includes index.
    ISBN 1-57851-600-5 (alk. paper)
    1. Marketing. 2. Telemarketing. 3. Marketing—Management. I. Jain,
D. (Dipak) II. Suvit Maesincee, 1961–   III. Title.

    HF5415 .K6313 2002
    658.8—dc21

                                 2001039445

From Philip Kotler
To my wife Nancy, my daughters, Amy, Melissa, and Jessica, and my sons-in-law, Joel, Steve, and Dan—with love.

From Dipak Jain
To my parents, my wife Sushant, and my children, Dhwani, Kalash, and Muskaan.

From Suvit Maesincee
To my wife Pagagrong and my daughters, Erica and Daral.

CONTENTS

PREFACE

Markets today are changing fast. Price-sensitive customers, new competitors, new distribution channels, new communication channels, the Internet, wireless commerce, globalization, deregulation, privatization . . . the list goes on. And it is not only markets that are changing, but the technologies that support them: e-commerce, e-mail, mobile phones, fax machines, sales and marketing automation, cable TV, videoconferencing. It is imperative that companies think through the revolutionary impact of these new technologies.

Companies also need to think through the opportunities and perils of globalization. Foreign markets are a source of lower-cost goods for production and a market for a company's brands. At the same time they pose risks due to differences in laws, language, business objectives, and supply systems.

Today's major economic problem is overcapacity in most of the world's industries. Customers are scarce, not products. Demand, not supply, is the problem. Overcapacity leads to hypercompetition, with too many goods chasing too few customers. And most goods and services lack differentiation. The result: dog-eat-dog pricing and mounting business failures.

The Internet, technology, and globalization have combined to create a new economy. The *old economy* is built on the logic of managing *manufacturing industries*; the *new economy* is built on the logic of managing information and *information industries*. The new economy holds that those competitors with the best information systems and intelligence will be the winners. Not surprisingly, many companies are quickly digitizing their businesses to achieve cost savings and increased market reach and penetration.

The Internet has given new capabilities to both consumers and producers. Previously the company had been the hunter searching for customers; now the consumer has become the hunter. The consumer informs the company of his specific requirements, proposes the price he will pay, establishes how he wants to receive the goods, and decides whether he will give permission to receive company information and advertising.

The old economy is not gone, however. Today's economy is a mix of the old economy and the new economy. Companies need to retain most of their skills and competencies that have worked in the past. But they also need to acquire new mind-sets and competencies if they hope to prosper in the future.

The bottom line is that markets are changing faster than our marketing. The classic marketing model needs to be future-fitted. Marketing must be deconstructed, redefined, and stretched. Marketing is not going to work if its only charge is to pump up the sales of existing goods (i.e., traditional *make-and-sell* marketing). Marketers need to get more involved in deciding what goods to pump *out*. Smart firms are adopting a *sense-and-respond* marketing mind-set.

Today's businesses must strive to satisfy customers' needs in the most convenient way, minimizing the time and energy that customers spend in searching for, ordering, and receiving goods and services. Businesses must make better use of their collaborators (e.g., suppliers, distributors, employees, and community) if they hope to ensure that their customers' needs are fulfilled more satisfactorily and more cost effectively. Businesses must deal with the two fundamental forces affecting businesses: *supply-side commoditization* and *demand-side customization*.

Businesses need to shift from focusing on their *product portfolios* to focusing on their *customer portfolios*. Today's marketing is increasingly about *customer relationship management*. Companies need skills in measuring customer profitability and customer lifetime value, in upselling and cross-selling, and in data mining customer databases and customizing messages and offerings.

Marketing strategy must be developed in the context of *corporate strategy.* Marketing integrates the work of creating and delivering customer value and must have more influence on the rest of the organization. We hold that marketing should be positioned as the driver of corporate strategy in the digital economy. Companies need a new corporate and marketing mind-set to perform successfully in the digital age.

Marketing Moves presents a new framework for conducting marketing strategy and operations. We replace the *selling concept,* and the later *marketing concept,* with the *holistic marketing concept.* Our framework calls for integrating three types of management: *demand management, resource management,* and *network management.* By doing this, the company can conduct its marketing activities on four platforms: *market offerings, marketing activities, business architecture,* and *operational systems.* Market offerings and business architecture can be viewed as the revenue drivers, while marketing activities and operational systems can be viewed as the cost drivers. Holistic marketers succeed by developing and managing a superior value network where the inputs to the offering and all the outputs are integrated and delivered at a high level of quality, service, and speed.

We hope that this book will help companies with the following classic tasks:

• Identifying new value opportunities for renewing their markets

• Efficiently creating the more promising new value offerings

• Using their capabilities and infrastructure to deliver the new value offerings efficiently

ACKNOWLEDGMENTS

Many companies and individuals helped us think through marketing's role in the new economy. We reviewed the latest new business ideas and practices of business leaders. We researched the latest work on customer relationship marketing, brand building, integrated marketing communications, supply chain management, and value creation and delivery. We developed our ideas and created a new framework for how marketing should be practiced in the twenty-first century.

We thank these intellectual sources, and we thank the full-time marketing faculty of the Kellogg School of Management at Northwestern University: James C. Anderson, Robert C. Blattberg, Bobby J. Calder, Gregory S. Carpenter, Alexander Chernev, Anne Coughlan, Dawn M. Iacobucci, Lakshman Krishnamurthi, Robert Kozinets, Angela Lee, Christie L. Nordhielm, Mohanbir S. Sawhney, John F. Sherry, Louis W. Stern, Brian Sternthal, Alice M. Tybout, Andris A. Zoltners. We had numerous discussions on various ideas over the years with all of these people, and their insights helped us develop this new marketing framework.

We also thank the following persons for the assistance they gave us in preparing this book: Tulikaa Khunnah and Siddhartha Singh, Ph.D. students in the Kellogg School Marketing Department. Also a special thanks goes to Kirsten Sandberg, Barbara Roth, and Amanda Elkin of the Harvard Business School Press for their valuable suggestions and assistance.

Finally, we thank our family members for all their support and encouragement.

Philip Kotler
Dipak Jain
Suvit Maesincee

MARKETING
MOVES

Part One

RESHAPING MARKETING FOR THE DIGITAL ECONOMY

ONE

Positioning Marketing as the Driver in the Digital Economy

Business and marketing strategy are undergoing a sea change. Consider the statements of some of America's business leaders:

> *Every now and then, a technology or an idea comes along that is so profound, so powerful, so universal that its impact changes everything. The printing press. The incandescent light. The automobile. Manned flight. It doesn't happen often, but when it does, the world is changed forever.*[1]
>
> —Lou Gerstner, Chairman of IBM

> *Embrace the Internet. Bring me a plan as to how you are going to transform your business beyond adding an Internet site.*[2]
>
> —Jack Welch, former CEO of GE

> *The Internet is not just another sales channel. It's not just an advertising medium. It is a tool to change fundamentally how a company does business and how it takes orders from its customers and provides value to them.*[3]
>
> —Esther Dyson, Chairman of EDventure Holdings Inc.

These business leaders are focusing on the potential impact of the Internet on future market and business behavior. But the Internet, with its underpinnings in digitalization and networks, is only one of several *technological* advances dramatically reshaping markets and businesses. Others include biotechnology, new materials, new medical treatments, new communication advances, and smart chips. *Globalization* is another major force affecting our lives. Consumers around the world are exposed to new ways of living and consuming and want many of the things they see. And a growing number of companies are responding by expanding their global reach to satisfy the new appetites. *Deregulation* and *privatization* are additional forces opening up markets and creating vast new opportunities.

These changes have made it fashionable for observers to talk in terms of the "old economy" and the "new economy." They see the *old economy* as having been built on the logic of managing *manufacturing industries.* Manufacturers apply certain principles and practices for the successful operation of their factories. They try to standardize their products in order to bring down their costs. They continually seek to expand their market and organizational size in order to achieve economies of scale. If they operate in different markets, they tend to replicate their procedures and their outlets. Their guiding principle is to achieve efficiency. And to accomplish this, they manage their firms *hierarchically,* with a boss on top issuing orders to middle managers who in turn guide the workers. These organizations tend to be centralized and highly controlled by rules.

The *new economy* (also referred to as the *digital economy*) is based on the digital revolution and the management of *information industries.* Information has a number of attributes. It can be infinitely differentiated, customized, and personalized. It can be dispatched to a great number of people who are on a network and can reach them quickly. To the extent that the information is made public and transparent, it will make people better informed and able to make better choices. New economy organizations tend to be flat, decentralized, and open to employee initiative.

Today's economy is a hybrid of the old and the new. It could appropriately be called the "now" or the "next" economy. Lou Gerstner of IBM recently recanted his statement quoted at the beginning of this chapter, saying, "There is no new economy. . . . The wars haven't changed; it's just that somebody has invented gunpowder."[4]

Companies need to retain most of the skills and competencies that have made them successful in the past. But if they hope to grow and prosper in today's economy, they will need to develop major new understandings and competencies. They must fundamentally rethink and revise their *corporate strategies,* aligning them with their marketing strategies, and they will have to rethink marketing's role within corporate strategy. In this book, we argue that companies will have to institute a more holistic marketing process for exploring, creating, and delivering value in order to continuously renew their markets. We particularly emphasize that marketing must play the lead role in shaping this new strategy.

This is not the first time that U.S. companies have had to change their corporate mind-set. Years ago, when the American public recognized the outstanding quality of many Japanese and European products, U.S. companies scrambled to upgrade their quality standards and manufacturing performance. They assimilated new ideas about total quality management, benchmarking, outsourcing, faster cycle time, and reengineering. The task of company transformation was placed in the hands of company engineers and manufacturing people.

The advent of the information age has required another corporate mind-set shift. Companies have had to invest heavily in information technology and network connectivity. Their investment in information technology has far exceeded their investment in plants and equipment. With the sudden rise of "pure-click" e-commerce dot-coms in the 1990s, most established companies were taken by surprise.

They watched these upstarts create a whole new *marketspace*—a virtual marketplace—for commercial transactions. They were dumbfounded by the skyrocketing market capitalizations of America Online, Amazon, Yahoo!, eBay, E*TRADE, and other dot-coms, many of which were worth more than Kodak, Gillette, American Airlines, and other corporate giants.

Relief came to these established companies when the dot-com bubble burst. Many new billionaires joined the "90-percent club," defined by those like Jay Walker, the founder of Priceline.com, who lost more than 90 percent of their wealth in the dot-com crash. Still, no companies expect marketspace to disappear. Indeed established companies are embracing the opposite view, that they are in the best position to leverage the Internet. Many are quickly incorporating e-commerce, e-procurement, e-recruitment, e-training, and other electronic pathways into their daily practices and procedures.

The information age has created hypercompetitive markets. Buyers are more aware of competitive offers, more price conscious, and more demanding than in the past. Power has migrated from the manufacturers and retailers to the consumers, who can now define what they want in the way of customized products and services, prices, distribution channels, and even advertising and sales promotion.

The digital economy has reached a stage at which companies must define their scope and the position of their markets more robustly. They need new marketing concepts, capabilities, and linkages that extend far beyond the boundaries of the conventional marketing department. Marketing must be made a greater force in the company's corporate strategy and organization. This is the next transformation imperative determining the fate of companies in the new economy.

In this chapter, we will first look at the major shifts that are creating the digital economy as they redraw industry boundaries and empower consumers. We summarize the resulting new capabilities now in the hands of consumers and business firms. We then discuss how the business mind-set is migrating from old ideas to new ones. We will show how marketing is changing within the context of the digital economy. Finally, we will spell out the framework for the new holistic marketing concept.

MAJOR SHIFTS TOWARD THE DIGITAL ECONOMY

Firms must make nine major shifts in their business and marketing thinking if they are to operate successfully in the digital economy.

- From asymmetry of information to the democratization of information

- From goods for elites to goods for everyone

- From make-and-sell to sense-and-respond

- From local economy to global economy

- From the economics of diminishing returns to the economics of increasing returns

- From owning assets to gaining access

- From corporate governance to market governance

- From mass markets to markets of one

- From just-in-time to real-time

From Asymmetry of Information to the Democratization of Information

Economists argue that markets are the best mechanism to allocate resources, provided that there is perfect and symmetric information, as well as equality of market power and mobility among individual agents. These assumptions, however, do not always hold in the real world. Sellers typically have access to better information than do consumers. Customers tend to be relatively ill informed, information is marketer controlled, and exchanges are marketer initiated. The result is *monopolistic competition,* in which sellers set the terms while consumers rely on such factors as brand recognition, company reputation, and endless advertising.

Digital technologies are drastically changing this information and power imbalance. More sellers are participating in the Internet marketspace because of its low barriers to entry. More customers can retrieve information about any product, service, or company. Information is ubiquitous and cheap.

Companies, as well as consumers, benefit from the information revolution. Using e-procurement, companies can compare supplier prices and lower their purchasing costs. By setting up extranets with their suppliers and distributors, they can lower their ordering, transaction, and payment costs. They are better able to assess demand and supply conditions. They can then use dynamic algorithms to adjust their prices and outputs, resulting in more efficient resource management.[5]

From Goods for Elites to Goods for Everyone

In the old economy, companies found it too expensive to give individual customers exactly what they wanted. Customers faced a trade-off between goods that were approximately right but relatively cheap and ones that were exactly right but expensive. Wealthy people could access more customized products or services.

In the new economy, many more people can access customized goods and services. Digital technology has lowered the costs of manufacturing "batches of one." We are seeing evidence of this on Web sites such as Dell.com (computers), Acumins.com (vitamins), IC3D.com (blue jeans), and Sonic.com (customized CDs). The drivers are the creation of a global, standardized communications infrastructure; the Internet; and the Web browser. Professor Ward Hanson sees customization as leading to a "democracy of goods."[6]

From Make-and-Sell to Sense-and-Respond

Make-and-sell has long been the dominant paradigm in business. Make-and-sell companies compete by estimating market demand, planning production, and building up inventory to match supply and demand. They rely primarily on achieving economies of scale, speeding up employees' learning curves, and executing defined procedures in accordance with a prescribed business plan.

Today, many companies compete by a *sense-and-respond* paradigm. Sense-and-respond companies invite customers to define their broad needs and even participate in choosing the exact attributes they want; they trigger their activities in response to orders; and they use digital technology to fill orders quickly. Sense-and-respond companies are superior to make-and-sell companies because they:[7]

- stimulate the development of more original products,

- produce technically superior products more quickly,

- become more customer-centric and fulfill consumer needs more effectively, and

- lead to higher profitability

From Local Economy to Global Economy

The Internet permits companies to expand their geographical reach exponentially. In the new economy, companies don't have to be big to be global. For the first time, small companies can reach prospects anywhere in the world. They can locate anywhere. And conversely, large companies with multiple geographical locations can reconsider how many locations they truly need. According to Robert Baldock:

> In industries such as textiles, direct selling has also had a big impact. With the help of multimedia aids like CD-ROMs, garment industry buyers in Europe and America are communicating directly with factories in India and the Far East, in many cases cutting out the need for an agent in those places. Designers in New York can send their latest designs electronically to factories in Asia where they are cut and sewn in quantities determined by orders that have in turn been gathered electronically from around the world and transmitted to the factory via the Internet. The only travel that needs to be done is by the garments themselves.[8]

Companies need to consider the consequences of international marketing via the Internet because it presents both advantages and disadvantages. The key enabling platforms have been the availability of logistics (e.g., FedEx services) and financial institutions (e.g., credit cards), which make international transactions as easy to conduct as local ones. Customers no longer have to buy from high-priced merchants in their own country if the same goods are available from low-priced merchants abroad. This situation may lead national governments to enact legislation to restrict using the Internet to order goods from abroad.[9]

From the Economics of Diminishing Returns to the Economics of Increasing Returns

Company growth in the industrial age was limited by the operation of the law of diminishing returns. Size brought bureaucracy, slower response time, and greater risk aversion. Market leaders defended their turf by attempting to control sources of supply, securing patents, and waging lawsuits against aggressive newcomers. Procter & Gamble, for instance, developed new products and product extensions to control shelf space, and The Home Depot attacked local hardware stores by offering greater variety at lower prices.

In the new economy, information explodes. Data can be replicated, stored, transferred, decomposed, and recombined in multiple ways. On the Internet, shelf space is unlimited. Shoppers can enter every site. Companies with limited resources can achieve tremendous scale in very little time.[10]

Growth in the new economy is governed by self-reinforcing cycles. Consider Metcalfe's law, which states that "the cost of the network expands linearly with increase in network size, but the value of the network increases exponentially."[11] Many e-businesses require a significant number of network members, and the member benefits will increase nonlinearly with a growing number of members. According to researchers for the McKenna group:

> Early in 1998 "ecompare.com" opened with no hint as to what it offered. Its owners left it to visitors to find out what was behind the entry page. They offered only one thing: Each visitor could register and receive ten free shares in the company. Within a few weeks, ecompare had more than three million registered users. From this "regular clientele," the company built up a virtual shopping network within a few months.[12]

In marketspace, a company must make a large up-front investment to create offerings and build networks, but the variable costs thereafter are relatively modest. Some products and services (e.g., information, music software) can be reproduced digitally and delivered electronically with essentially zero marginal cost. This negligible cost of increasing capacity, combined with the ubiquity of reach, stimulates a rapid growth in demand. Therefore, the new economy operates with increasing returns to scale.

In the new economy, companies must design strategies to exploit abundance. The first Internet company in an industry category that achieves a large customer base will tend to attract additional users at a much lower cost because of its visibility and word of mouth. Al Ries and Laura Ries go so far as to postulate a "Law of Singularity," which says that one Internet firm will own the category and all the others will trail hopelessly behind, if they exist at all.[13]

From Owning Assets to Gaining Access

In the new economy, firms are reevaluating whether they should own certain assets or simply access those assets only when needed through subscriptions, memberships, leases, and retainers. Bob Shapiro, Monsanto's CEO, highlighted this issue with his provocative question: "Why should anyone want to own anything anyway?"[14] The fact is, many corporations today compete on *access* to assets, not ownership of them. Ownership of physical property has actually become a liability. As a result, companies around the world have transformed themselves into "lean" organizations by *decapitalizing*—outsourcing activities, selling off physical assets, leasing equipment, and shrinking their working capital. Today, many companies would rather own a brand than a factory.

Consumers are also changing their role from product owners to product renters, such as by leasing rather than owning their cars and renting everything from software to furnaces.[15] Consider what Renault today is offering to prospective car buyers.

> *Renault offers a package of services as part of the initial leasing price. It is effectively "lending" customers the car, freeing them of all the usual hassles of ownership over the contract, and charging for that lending and the care and the services. (The only thing the driver has to do is pay for the gas!) Renault believes that not only do customers*

get more value over the life of the vehicle this way, but it also costs them less and Renault plans to gain by using this approach to become a permanent feature over the customer's entire driving life.[16]

From Corporate Governance to Market Governance

Companies incur transaction costs whenever they acquire products or services outside instead of making them internally. *Transaction costs* include search costs—the time, money, and resources consumed in locating the best suppliers and deals. By using intermediaries to provide product information, companies could reduce, but not eliminate, such search costs. *Contracting costs* are incurred when the exchange requires a unique or an extended price negotiation and contract. Finally, there are the *costs of coordinating resources and processes.*

According to Ronald Coase, "a firm will tend to expand until the costs of organizing an extra transaction within the firm become equal to the costs of carrying out the same transaction on the open market."[17] Companies will perform in-house those activities that have a cost advantage and will outsource other activities.

The information revolution has put companies in a better position to coordinate complex activities and make decisions. The increased availability of information has reduced transaction costs. More transactions are shifting from companies' existing hierarchical coordination to market coordination. More transactions will be conducted electronically. As transaction and coordination costs fall, e-markets and e-intermediaries will become pivotal.

Companies are increasingly focusing on their customers and core competencies and outsourcing other activities. Success in today's markets requires developing strong relationships with customers, suppliers, and business partners. Skill in customer relationship building and management is an increasingly important capability.[18]

From Mass Markets to Markets of One

In the new economy, marketing is fundamentally reversed from finding customers for products to finding products for customers. Digital technology enables companies to track each customer, turning traditional *one-to-many marketing* into *one-to-one marketing*. According to Martha Rogers and Don Peppers, one-to-one companies gather information about, and communicate directly with, individuals to form ongoing, intimate business relationships.[19]

All real-time drivers—speed, value chain integration, new infomediaries—enable companies to practice one-to-one marketing, not necessarily capital-intensive or scale-based operations. The best small businesses are able to enjoy one-to-one relationships with their customers. Think about your neighborhood bookstore: "Good to see you, Mary. Did you enjoy that biography of Thomas Jefferson I recommended? Great! Then you might appreciate this new book on Churchill that I put aside for you." This kind of personal interest makes any consumer feel special.[20]

From Just-in-Time to Real-Time

With the increased availability and speed of information, companies gain a near real-time, undistorted view of demand. They can respond quickly and link tightly to markets, matching supply with demand. Information has replaced physical inventory, unleashing a major restructuring of the supply chain. Consider the following examples:

- Wal-Mart captures precise information about its inventory and daily sales of thousands of its stock-keeping units, makes this information transparent to its major suppliers such as Procter & Gamble, and lets P&G figure out how many cases of diapers, detergents, and toothpaste to ship to each of Wal-Mart's stores every day.

• Dell Computer builds a computer when it gets an order. In 1999, this strategy reduced Dell's inventory period from an industry average of 60–70 days to just 6 days and increased Dell's inventory turnover to 58–60 times a year as compared with 13.5 for Compaq and 9.8 for IBM's PC business.[21]

• Cisco owns only 2 of the 40 factories that manufacture its branded products. Cisco relays orders for routers and other Internet items to its supplier partners, who manufacture its branded products.

Many suppliers are not set up to fulfill small orders on a daily or an hourly basis. They must acquire this capability in order to minimize their inventory levels.[22]

These major shifts have opened up an entirely new set of consumer and business capabilities, which we explain below.

CONSUMERS AND BUSINESSES ACQUIRE NEW CAPABILITIES

New Consumer Capabilities

The digital revolution has given buyers several new capabilities:

• *A substantial increase in buyer power.* Buyers today can compare prices and product attributes in a matter of seconds. They are only a click away from comparing competitors' prices on such Web sites as mySimon.com and Buy.com. On Priceline.com, consumers can even name the price they want to pay for a hotel room, an airline ticket, or a mortgage and see whether any willing suppliers respond. Business buyers can run a reverse auction, in which sellers compete during a given time period to underprice one another in order to capture the buyer's business. Buyers can join with others to aggregate their purchases and thereby achieve deeper volume discounts (for example, through DailyeDeals.com).

- *A greater variety of available goods and services.* Amazon advertises itself as the world's largest bookstore, with more than three million books in print. No physical bookstore can match that inventory. Today a person can order almost anything over the Internet: furniture (ethanallen.com), washing machines (sears.com), management consulting (ernie.ey.com), medical advice (cyberdocs .com), and so on. Furthermore, buyers can order these goods and services from anywhere in the world, which helps people living in countries with very limited local offerings to achieve great savings. It also means that buyers in countries with high prices can reduce their costs by ordering elsewhere.

- *A great amount of information about practically anything.* Today's consumers can buy almost any newspaper in any language from anywhere in the world. They also have access to online encyclopedias, dictionaries, medical information, movie ratings, consumer reports, and countless other information sources.

- *An increased ability to interact with vendors when placing and receiving orders.* Now buyers can place orders from their homes and offices twenty-four hours a day, seven days a week. And the orders will be delivered directly to them so they have no need to travel, park, and stand in store lines.

- *A leveraged ability to chat with other buyers and compare notes.* Today's consumers can enter a chat room about an area of common interest and exchange information and opinions. Women, for example, can visit iVillage.com to discuss child-rearing issues; movie lovers can visit any number of movie chat rooms to talk about films.

New Business Capabilities

Today's companies have also benefited from new capabilities ushered in by the Internet.

- *Companies can add a powerful new information and sales source with extended geographical reach to inform customers and to promote their products and services.* By establishing one or more company Web sites, companies can describe their products and services, relate their histories, explain their business philosophies, list their job opportunities, and provide other information of interest to viewers. In the past, companies were limited for *financial reasons* in the amount of information they could send in the form of ads, brochures, and so on. Today, the Internet permits transmitting an almost unlimited amount of rich information. By putting their extensive catalogs on their Web sites, companies such as Grainger have facilitated their customers' search and ordering processes. Each company has the option of turning its Web site into a sales channel as well as an information channel. Furthermore, since the Internet is ubiquitous, people from anywhere in the world can learn about and possibly order goods from the company.

- *Companies can facilitate two-way communication with their customers and prospects as well as expedite transactions.* The Internet makes it easy for individuals to send e-mail messages to companies and receive replies. And companies are developing *extranets* with their suppliers and distributors for sending and receiving information, orders, and payments more efficiently. In addition, they can conduct marketing research using the Internet. They can run focus groups, set up customer panels, and send out questionnaires to gather primary data. Companies can send their customers and prospects marketing materials via e-mail. Companies are now able to send coupons (e.g., coolsavings.com), samples (e.g., freesamples.com), e-mail offers, and information to customers who have requested these items or have given the company permission to send them.

- *Companies can customize their offerings and services to individual customers.* Companies can track the number of visitors to their Web sites and the frequency of their visits. By putting this information into their customer databases, and enhancing it with other information, they are better positioned to target individual customers and prospects and thus to individualize their messages, offerings, and services accordingly.

- *Companies can improve their purchasing, recruiting, training, and internal and external communication.* All companies are buyers as well as sellers. Companies are achieving substantial savings by using the Internet to compare sellers' prices and to purchase inputs at auctions or on digital marketplaces or by posting their own terms. Companies are also preparing and posting password-protected training products on the Internet that their employees, dealers, and agents can download so that they don't have to attend classes to be kept up-to-date.

These new capabilities available to buyers and sellers alike have the potential of greatly enhancing marketplace efficiency and performance.

MATCHING CAPABILITIES WITH VALUE DRIVERS

These capabilities dramatically change the configuration of markets. In the digital economy, every business comprises two kinds of markets—the physical market, namely the *marketplace,* and the virtual market, namely the *marketspace.* Driven by the Internet and digital technology, most businesses—including banking, insurance, and travel agencies—have added a marketspace presence to their marketplace presence.

We see three major drivers shaping today's markets: customer value, core competencies, and collaborative networks (see table 1-1).

Customer Value

The nine major shifts and the new consumer and business capabilities dramatically change the philosophy of business from being *product-centric* to *customer-centric*.

Operate as a customer-centric company. Companies are recognizing that it is more valuable to own customers than products, physical

---

TABLE 1-1 Drivers for Mastering the Value Stream in the New Business Landscape

Value Driver	Business Imperative
Customer value	• Operate as a customer-centric company • Focus on customer value and satisfaction • Develop distribution channels matched to customer preference • Develop and manage with a marketing scorecard • Make profits on customer lifetime value
Core competencies	• Outsource those activities that others can do better, faster, or cheaper • Benchmark against "best practices" around the world • Keep inventing new competitive advantages • Operate with cross-departmental teams that manage processes • Operate in marketspace as well as in the marketplace
Collaborative networks	• Focus on balancing stakeholder interests • Be generous in rewarding the company's partners • Use fewer suppliers and turn them into partners

plants, or equipment. Nike doesn't produce its own shoes; Sarah Lee outsources much of its manufacturing. Companies no longer think of customers as buying only one of their products. Rather, they are building product lines that will allow them to cross-sell several items to their current customers. Organizationally, the company's product people should be viewed as suppliers to customer group managers, who would even have the right to source products elsewhere if internal supply costs are too high. The challenge is for customer managers to learn what customers want and to arrange for appropriate product assortments.

Focus on customer value and satisfaction. Companies can often make more money in the short run by high-pressure selling. To close a deal, many salespeople will over-promise and under-deliver. But these tactics lead to disappointed customers, increased customer turnover, and high costs for finding new customers. Smart companies develop brands that make a promise to the customer and then deliver on the promise. They go further, continuously searching for new value to add to their customers' operations and satisfaction.

Develop distribution channels matched to customer preferences. Companies often retain and protect one form of distribution despite customers' wishes to obtain the product in a different way. For example, many people would like to buy cars without going to a car dealer, by ordering the car from a catalog or over the Internet as one might order a Dell computer. Yet auto companies are heavily invested in their dealerships and so are not very free to establish direct sales channels that would compete with their dealers. But when consumer pressure mounts sufficiently and just one company challenges the established distribution channel, change will be inevitable. In the long run, customer distribution preferences will prevail.

Develop and manage with a marketing scorecard. Top management guides its business largely by its *financial scorecards,* namely its P&L statement and its balance sheet. But the company's performance is the result of actions in the marketplace. Companies would be smart to prepare a *marketing scorecard* that would track market-based variables such as share of mind, customer satisfaction, customer loss rate, relative product quality, and other measures that alert management to impending company challenges and opportunities.

Make profits on customer lifetime value. Companies need to think beyond just making a sale. They must think about a customer's lifetime value, namely the present value of the expected future profit from the customer. They must think about how to gain a greater share of the customer's business within a category. The aim is to deliver more long-term value for the customer and thus create a longer-lasting customer.

In the digital economy, competitive advantage derives more from relational capital and less from traditional physical capital. Companies focus as much on growing their share of each customer's business as on growing their share of market. Capturing a large market share is not necessarily equivalent to having many loyal customers. In fact, a company might maintain its market share but at the same time lose and replace a significant percentage of its customers at great expense. But by focusing on enlarging customer share, companies will be led to redefine their product mix, service mix, distribution mix, and communication mix. Instead of acting as hunters, smart companies perform as gardeners, nurturing their customers.[23]

Core Competencies

The second driver in today's business landscape is core competencies. In the analog economy, most companies operate three different businesses: a product innovation and commercialization business, a customer relationships business, and an operations and infrastructure business. In the context of the digital economy, each business has different economics and each requires different skill sets. The nine major shifts and new capabilities have substantially changed the mind-set of business from "make it big" and "make it better" to "make it fast" and "make it different."

Outsource those activities that others can do better, faster, or cheaper. No company can conduct all its activities with superior competence. The days of Henry Ford wanting to own and operate everything that goes into the making of a car—including tire manufacturing, seat manufacturing, and glass manufacturing—are over. Companies are willing to turn over non-core activities to outsourcers who can perform them more efficiently.

Benchmark against "best practices" around the world. At the very least, companies need to measure their performance against their competitors' performance levels. But companies can also learn a great deal by observing businesses outside their industry that have great reputations for superbly conducting one or more activities. Companies can visit 3M to learn about innovation, Disney to learn about training service-oriented employees, FedEx to learn about logistics, and L.L. Bean to learn about great customer service.

Keep inventing new competitive advantages. Professor Michael Porter of Harvard Business School urges companies to develop a sustainable competitive advantage. Every company would like to achieve such an advantage, but in this rapidly changing world, no advantage lasts for long. Competitors are quick to copy it, thus reducing its power. Companies must be in the business of continuously searching for and inventing new value for customers by recognizing and responding to changing customer needs and values.

Operate with cross-departmental teams that manage processes. For hundreds of years, companies have conducted their activities in discrete departments. Functional specialization creates departmental efficiency, but it also creates poor interdepartmental communication and coordination as well as power conflicts. The contribution of Michael Hammer and James Champy's *Reengineering the Corporation* was to shift our attention from company *functions* to company *processes*. Processes are larger in scope and more fundamental than functions and are set up to deliver outcomes that customers value. Examples of processes include the new-product development process, the order-to-payment process, and the customer acquisition and retention process. Processes normally require inputs from two or more departments. Companies are creating multidepartmental process teams to manage each process and run it so that it works smoothly in the customer's interests. Reengineering aims to break down the walls that normally separate each department.

Operate in marketspace as well as in the marketplace. Companies today recognize the advantage of developing Web sites to provide information about their company and promote their offerings. Some even turn their Web sites into direct sales channels. Companies with a heavy reliance on retailers, however, have less latitude in selling over the Internet. Retailers do not welcome competition from their suppliers and, faced with such competition, might threaten to drop the companies' products. Even if companies decide against using the Internet as a sales channel, they need to use marketspace for procurement, recruiting, training, internal communications, and information gathering at the very least.

Collaborative Networks

The third driver in today's markets is collaborative networks. Industrial-age giant corporations like General Motors, Ford, General Electric, and Standard Oil were enchanted with the idea of *vertical integration.* In response to the high transaction cost of building and maintaining linkages outside their corporate boundaries, they sought to link the disparate elements of the value chain under common ownership. The focused processes across the internal supply chain made it seem cheaper to make than to buy supplies.

The nine major shifts and new capabilities have made it increasingly feasible to replace vertical integration with *virtual integration.* Virtual information exchange reduces the time and staff size required to consummate transactions and coordinate activities across business entities.

A *collaborative network* consists of a company and the supporting stakeholders with which it has built mutually profitable business relationships. Increasingly, in the new economy, competition is not between companies but rather between collaborative networks, with the prize going to the company that has built the better network.

Focus on balancing stakeholder interests. Companies exist to serve the interest of their shareholders. But companies are coming to recognize that serving their shareholders may first involve serving their stakeholders well. Bill Marriott, Jr., puts the Marriott Corporation's priorities in this order: "First satisfy the employees; then they will satisfy our guests; then our guests will return frequently and this will make money for the stockholders."[24] Paul Allaire, chairman and CEO of Xerox, maintains that, if you satisfy your customers, employees, and partners, then profits will follow.

Be generous in rewarding the company's partners. There was a time when companies thought that they could make the most money by paying the least to their employees, suppliers, and distributors. This mind-set assumes a zero-sum game: the company gains the most by paying out the least. Today, we recognize that employees, suppliers, and distributors work harder when they are well paid and make the pie larger.

Many of the most profitable companies are very generous to their partners.

Use fewer suppliers and turn them into partners. Companies traditionally preferred to buy from several suppliers, making them compete for the companies' business. In the process, the companies could wrest concessions and hold down costs. Yet companies failed to appreciate the high costs of doing business in this way: Each supplier had to be monitored; product quality varied from supplier to supplier; and no supplier invested much, knowing that it might be replaced by another supplier. Finally, companies began to recognize the advantages of using fewer but better suppliers and turning them into partners who would invest more, participate in product design decisions, and be dependable even during periods of shortages.

THE NEED FOR A NEW MARKETING PARADIGM

The three value drivers—customer value, core competencies, and collaborative networks—are leading to a new marketing paradigm. This paradigm has evolved through two stages and is about to move into the third, as shown in table 1-2.

Under the *selling concept,* a company's task was to sell and promote the products coming out of its factories in an effort to win as much volume, and therefore profits, as possible. The job was to hunt down prospects wherever they could be found and use the mass-persuasion power of advertising and the individual-persuasion power of personal selling to make a sale. Management gave little thought to segmenting the market and developing different product and service versions that met the varying needs in the marketplace. The success mantra was product standardization followed by mass production, distribution, and marketing.

TABLE 1-2 The Three Stages of a New Marketing Paradigm

Name	Starting Point	Focus	Means	Ends
Selling concept	Factory	Products	Selling and promoting	Profits through sales volume
Marketing concept	Customers' varying needs	Appropriate offerings and marketing mixes	Market segmentation, targeting, and positioning	Profits through customer satisfaction
Holistic marketing concept	Individual customer requirements	Customer value, company's core competencies, and collaborative network	Database management and value chain integration linking collaborators	Profitable growth through capturing customer share, customer loyalty, and customer lifetime value

The *marketing concept* shifted the company's attention from the factory to customers and to their varying needs. Now, a company's aim was to develop appropriate segment-based offerings and marketing mixes. Companies refined their skills in market segmentation, targeting, and positioning. Delivering high customer satisfaction in each chosen segment would produce loyal customers whose repeat purchasing would lead to an upward spiral of high profits.

The *holistic marketing concept* represents a broadening of the marketing concept, made possible by the digital revolution. It is a dynamic concept derived from the electronic connectivity and interactivity among the company, its customers, and its collaborators. It integrates the value exploration, value creation, and value delivery activities with the purpose of building long-term, mutually satisfying relationships and co-prosperity among these key stakeholders.

Under the holistic marketing concept, the starting point is individual customer requirements. Marketing's task is to develop contextual offerings of products, services, and experiences to match individual customers' requirements. To explore, create, and deliver individual customer value in a very dynamic and competitive environment, marketers need to invest in the company's relational capital covering all stakeholders—consumers, collaborators, employees, and communities. Companies therefore go beyond the business concept of *customer relationship management* toward the concept of *whole relationship management.* Marketers constantly renew the market by building and managing a customer database and delivering value, with the help of collaborators linked together in a value network. Holistic marketers succeed by managing a superior value chain that delivers a high level of product quality, service, and speed. Holistic marketers achieve profitable growth by expanding customer share, building customer loyalty, and capturing customer lifetime value. We examine the shifts in marketing thinking in chapter 2.

THE HOLISTIC MARKETING FRAMEWORK

The holistic marketing framework enables management to answer the following questions:

- How can a company identify new value opportunities for renewing its markets?

- How can a company efficiently create the more promising new value offerings?

- How can a company use its capabilities and infrastructure to deliver the new value offerings efficiently?

Values emerge and flow within and across markets. Because markets are dynamic and competitive, management needs a well-defined strategy for value exploration. Developing such a strategy requires understanding the connections and interactions among three spaces: (1) the customer's cognitive space, (2) the company's competency space, and (3) the collaborator's resource space. In chapter 3 we examine how a company can use value exploration to renew its markets.

To exploit a value opportunity, the company needs value creation skills. Marketers need to: (1) identify new customer benefits from the customer's cognitive space, (2) utilize core competencies from its business domain, and (3) select and manage business partners from its collaborative network. We examine how marketers identify and create new market offerings in chapter 4.

To be able to deliver value requires substantial investment in infrastructure and capabilities. The company must become proficient at (1) customer relationship management, (2) internal resource management, and (3) business partnership management. *Customer relationship management* allows the company to discover who its customers are, how they behave, and what they need or want. It also enables the company to respond appropriately, coherently, and quickly to different customer opportunities. To respond effectively, the company requires *internal resource management* to integrate major business processes (e.g., order processing, general ledger, payroll, and production) within a single family of software modules. Finally, *business partnership management* allows the company to handle complex relationships with its trading partners to source, process, and deliver products. We will examine the value delivery requirements in chapter 6.

To create, maintain, and renew their business, companies can utilize the holistic marketing framework shown in figure 1-1. This framework shows the connection and interaction between relevant actors (customers, company, and collaborators) and value-based activities (value exploration, value creation, and value delivery).

FIGURE 1-1 A Holistic Marketing Framework

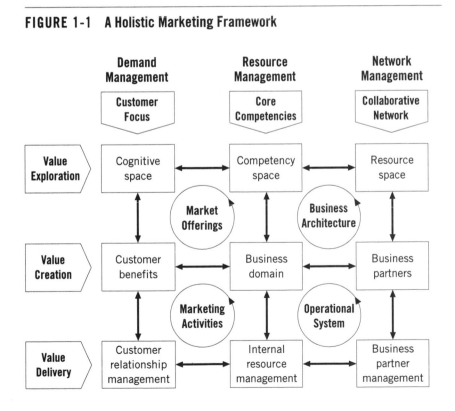

The holistic marketing framework provides guidance for reconfiguring a company's current organizational structure. Three organizational functions will play the major roles in the digital economy—the demand management function, the resource management function, and the network management function. The framework shows the high-level process of each of the three major functions. For example, the process along the demand management function starts with assessing the customer's cognitive space, then progresses to identifying customer benefits, and ends with building the relationship with the customer. The framework provides management with insight into ways of improving a company's organizational structure. We examine a company's organizational architecture in chapter 9.

CRAFTING THE COMPETITIVE PLATFORMS

Companies need platforms for exploring, creating, and delivering value. The nine building blocks in the holistic marketing framework constitute a strategic foundation for crafting four key competitive platforms for establishing corporate and business strategies.

1. *Market offerings platform.* The first set of basic building blocks—cognitive space, competency space, customer benefits, and business domain—give management strategic insight for developing market offerings. We will examine the market offerings platform in chapter 4.

2. *Business architecture platform.* The next set of basic building blocks—competency space, resource space, business domain, and business partners—guides management in reconfiguring the business architecture, which is made up of several value chains. We will examine the business architecture platform detail in chapter 5.

3. *Marketing activities platform.* The next set of basic building blocks—customer benefits, business domain, customer relationship management, and internal resource management—helps management to formulate its marketing activities to support the market offerings. We examine the marketing activities platform in chapter 7.

4. *Operational system platform.* The final set of basic building blocks—business domain, business partners, internal resource management, and business partnership management—provides strategic insight for designing the operational system. We examine the operational system platform in chapter 8.

To master the value stream, the three major functions—demand management, resource management, and network management—will work closely as cross-functional teams to drive a corporate and business strategy based on these four competitive platforms.

We argue that the outputs from the four platforms—market offerings, marketing activities, business architecture, and operational systems—provide the basis for corporate and business strategy (see figure 1-2). Companies need a well-defined corporate and business strategy to drive profitability and hence increase shareholder value.

FIGURE 1-2   Four Competitive Platforms That Deliver Value

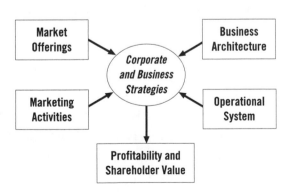

In arithmetic terms, profit = revenue − cost. The market offerings and business architecture can be viewed as the revenue drivers, while marketing activities and operational systems can be viewed as the cost drivers. We examine the profit drivers for business in the digital economy in chapter 9.

CONCLUSION

The central purpose of traditional marketing has been to sell products. The aim was to find customers for the company's products. Lester Wunderman, of direct marketing fame, has put it well: "The call of the Industrial Revolution, 'This is what I make, won't you please buy it?' will give way to that of the Consumer Revolution which will declare, 'This is what I need, can't you please make it?'"[25]

Today, the consumer is king. Whereas previously the company had been the hunter searching for customers, now the consumer has become the hunter. The consumer informs the company of his specific requirements, proposes the price he will pay, establishes how he wants to receive the goods, and decides whether he will give permission to receive company information and advertising.

Companies therefore must turn from a make-and-sell philosophy to a sense-and-respond philosophy. Businesses must take a larger view of the customers' value function and aim to satisfy customers' needs in the most convenient way, minimizing the time and energy that customers spend in searching for, ordering, and receiving goods and services. Businesses must make better use of their collaborators (e.g., suppliers, distributors, employees, and community) if they hope to ensure that their customers' needs are fulfilled more satisfactorily and more cost effectively. Businesses must acknowledge two fundamental forces in businesses: supply-side commoditization of products and services and demand-side customization.[26]

QUESTIONS TO PONDER

- How have each of the nine major shifts affected your company?

- Which of the new seller capabilities brought about by the Internet is your company exploiting?

- What initiatives has your company already taken to move toward a more holistic perspective? What remains to be done?

Formulating
a Market Renewal
Strategy

The holistic marketing process involves all stakeholders and requires them to participate in the value-creation process. In the digital economy, companies, customers, collaborators, and communities can drive values. Ideas can come from exploring the customer's cognitive space, the company's competency space, and the collaborators' resource space.

MASTERING VALUE IN THE DIGITAL ECONOMY

Today, many companies believe that value is expandable and sharable. The more the partners share the value, the more they will get back. In the digital world, not only the company but also the consumers, collaborators, and communities are actively driving value. Here, we consider how each group drives value creation.

Company-Driven Markets

Sometimes a company is the main driver of new value. In many product and service areas, customers do not know what they will want tomorrow, so companies take the lead in innovation. They generate significant new products, services, and business formats; establish new price points; develop new channels; and raise service to new levels. Notable company driving firms are Sony, 3M, CNN, Charles Schwab, and FedEx.

Companies today can offer customized services to a large number of customers using the Internet. For example, customers of Entergy can get customized analysis of their bills and power usage, and customers who use American Express services can manage their financial investments personally.[1]

Creating new markets requires a different pattern of strategic thinking. Instead of looking within the traditional market boundaries, marketers can look holistically across them. Companies can systematically redefine their businesses by looking across substitute industries, strategic groups, buyer groups, complementary offerings, the functional-emotional orientation of an industry, and even time.[2]

Customer-Driven Markets

A critical aspect of creating a successful market is the ability to integrate the customer into every key process. Customers can use the Internet to tell marketers what they want. The customer specifies the needs and the business delivers. Thus, the customer changes roles from "consumer" to "prosumer." For example, Dell prosumers put together their dream computers by choosing exactly those features and services that satisfy their needs.[3] And soon it will be common for purchasers to design cars on computer screens, choosing not only predetermined options but options provided by a variety of manufacturers: a Honda engine in a Toyota body with Ford seats and interior.

Customers might even be able to watch their cars being assembled on a computer screen while their insurance and car payment terms are being tailored to their finances.[4]

We are also witnessing consumers becoming company subcontractors, as they use self-service offerings. Companies provide an environment in which customers can take an active part in designing the product to meet their requirements by exploring the various options on the companies' Web sites and seeking solutions. This is a win-win scenario. Companies reduce the cost of servicing the self-service customers as well as get those customers involved in the design process, which reduces the chances of their switching to a rival. And customers get access to tools for developing and tailoring the offering to suit their needs.[5]

Along with the prosumer idea comes the possibility of involving customers in improving companies' production and distribution operations. In evaluating prototype versions of their offerings, Yahoo! and Netscape, for example, invited numerous volunteers to beta test their offerings, and their feedback was invaluable in adapting the products to fulfill customers' needs. This was an efficient, inexpensive exercise leading to even more innovative customized solutions that increased customer loyalty.[6]

Collaborator-Driven Markets

The real power of the new business models lies in their recognition of the value that their partners can contribute. The partners not only help increase operational efficiency but also strengthen the company's value-creation capabilities. For example, utilities and appliance manufacturers might soon collaborate to bundle together all the services related to using refrigerators, such as rental and financing, maintenance service, and electricity, and to charge one monthly payment for this "refrigeration" service.[7]

Collaborators may play a major role in initiating knowledge creation in the marketspace. Consider the design and manufacturing of Boeing's 777. About 250 cross-functional teams—including personnel from suppliers and airlines in different locations—jointly created the jet. All were connected electronically, using CAD/CAM software. The result was a reduction not only in the cost of development but also in time to market.[8]

Sun Microsystems employs the same kind of collaboration. Sun is working with its five top suppliers to compress the procure-to-pay cycle and to provide two-way communication about changing competitive conditions. This initiative will be expanded to Sun's twenty top suppliers, who account for roughly 90 percent of its $5 billion annual spending.

Companies now prefer to work with fewer suppliers. Doing so facilitates information sharing, joint product development, and compliance. It also leads to inventory reduction and faster turnaround times. In the U.S. auto industry, for instance, the number of parts suppliers decreased from 30,000 in 1988 to 4,000 in 1998, and it is expected to drop below 3,000 by 2003.[9]

Community-Driven Markets

Today's marketers still focus on how to use advertising and other tools to influence each customer, ignoring the fact that purchasing many types of products is partly a social process. Purchasing involves not only a one-to-one interaction between the company and the customer but also many exchanges of information and influence among the people who surround that customer. The Internet has enabled consumers to communicate directly with one another through e-mail, videoconferencing, and online chat rooms. Consumers can share their opinions about products, services, experiences, and companies. They can form communities based around common interests. As customer communities form, power shifts from sellers to customers. Intrusive advertising gives way to peer-level information dissemination through discussions of the distinctive features of brands. Such information is perceived as more reliable and will trump information from sellers. Customers in the Internet age should be viewed as members of communities sharing similar product interests rather than as market segments.[10] Len Short, executive vice president of advertising and brand management at Charles Schwab, summed it up this way: "The idea that a critical part of marketing is word of mouth and validation from important personal relationships is absolutely key, and most marketers ignore it."[11]

In order to foster a feeling of community among its users, Amazon.com encourages them to chat with one another and to send in their own book reviews, which are published on Amazon's site. Many users of Java software have formed communities that contribute code and discuss standards. Members of these communities create their own content and help one another figure out how to use the company's products.[12]

A company can gain substantial information by initiating communities and participating in others. Brand-related communities, such as the Harley Davidson Riders' Club and communities for football team fans, are numerous. It should be noted, however, that customer-provided information may be available to competitors as well as to the company.[13]

Most customer communities are independent of company influence or participation. Areas of interest include finance (e.g., motleyfool.com), automotive (e.g., autoweb.com and edmunds.com), general goods (e.g., netmarket.com), water utilities (e.g., wateronline.com), and air pollution (e.g., pollutiononline.com). Consumers perceive these sites as credible mainly because they don't have links to the product and service providers that own them. The major challenge for these communities is to provide continuous value-added services and maintain member trust.[14]

SHIFTS IN STRATEGIC MARKETING

The four value-driving forces—companies, customers, collaborators, and communities—are significantly changing strategic marketing thinking and operational marketing. First consider the strategic shifts in marketing thinking shown in table 2-1.

Here are the main elements in the new strategic marketing mind-set.

- *Marketing integrates the work of creating and delivering customer value and must have more influence on the rest of the organization.* Marketing has traditionally been viewed as the department whose work was limited to planning and integrating the company's marketing activities. If the company achieved its sales goals, the department was well regarded; if the company failed to achieve its sales goals, the marketing department was to blame. The late David Packard, cofounder of Hewlett-Packard, had observed that "marketing is far too important to leave to the marketing department."[15] The implication was that a company could have the best marketing department in the world and still fail at marketing if other departments failed to act in the customers' interests. The

---

TABLE 2-1 Changing Assumptions in Strategic Marketing Thinking

Old Strategic Marketing	New Strategic Marketing
Marketing department does the marketing.	Marketing integrates the work of exploring, creating, and delivering customer value.
Marketer focuses on "interruption" marketing.	Marketer focuses on "permission" marketing.
Marketing focuses on acquiring new customers.	Marketing focuses on customer retention and loyalty building.
Marketing focuses on immediate transactions.	Marketing focuses on capturing customer lifetime value.
Marketing expenditures are viewed as expenses.	Many marketing expenditures are viewed as investments.

best-laid marketing plans would not succeed if the manufacturing group didn't create the right product, if the logistics people didn't deliver the product on time, if the accounting department didn't explain its bills properly, and if the telephone operators didn't provide helpful information to prospective buyers. Although marketing efforts are normally directed forward toward the middlemen (push) and the final consumers (pull), senior marketing executives must also direct their effort backward, to ensure that new product development designs the right products, purchasing buys the right inputs, manufacturing produces the right quality, and logistics delivers the products on time. Marketing must go beyond operating as a department. Marketing and customer-centric thinking must permeate the company's outlook, providing perspectives, principles, and practices intended to make customer value and satisfaction everyone's job.

• *Marketing focuses on permission marketing.* In the digital economy, consumers pull the information that they need and initiate exchanges. They increasingly stipulate the exchange terms. Even if customers visit a company's Web site, that company now must ask for and receive permission from individual customers or prospects in order to communicate and build a relationship with them. Accordingly, marketing perspectives and practices are changing from *interruption marketing* to *permission marketing.*

• *Marketing must focus on retaining customers and building loyalty.* Traditionally, the company's sales force devotes substantial time to acquiring new customers. The sales force heroes are those who have won important new accounts. But the flip side is a heightened danger of neglecting current customers. After all, a company can grow in two ways, either by finding new customers or by selling more to existing customers. Companies are now placing more emphasis on the latter. Managers are training their sales forces in customer relationship building, cross-selling, and up-selling as ways to increase growth.

- *Marketing focuses on capturing the lifetime value of the best customers.* Companies don't like to lose money on a transaction. They may begrudge times when a customer returns goods, requests a deeper discount, or requires special services. These episodes reduce the company's profits and may even create losses. But the correct vantage point is to view how profitable the customer might be over the long term. The company must accept occasional losses to preserve high lifetime value customers. Those customers with small or negative lifetime value can be treated differently. The company needs to raise its fees or lower its costs of serving less desirable customers. Either these actions will raise their lifetime value, or these customers will decide to exit at no great loss to the company.

- *Many marketing expenditures are, in fact, investments.* Companies tend to view marketing expenditures on the sales force, advertising, and sales promotion as expenses rather than asset-building investments. CEOs frequently cut marketing budgets toward the end of the year if profits are falling below expectations. Yet those slashes lead to cutbacks in communication, service, and on-time delivery, hobbling the company's ability to deliver promised value and satisfaction to the company's target customers. To illustrate the investment value of marketing expenditures, consider the vast amount of money Coca-Cola spends to advertise itself and to place its products within reach of everyone in the world. As a brand, Coca-Cola has an estimated market value of $70 billion. Who wouldn't prefer to own the Coca-Cola brand rather than Coca-Cola's physical assets? Marketing needs to be seen as an investment center whose expenditures create long-lasting customers and income flows. Only the current part of marketing costs should be expensed.

SHIFTS IN OPERATIONAL MARKETING

We anticipate a number of changes in the direction of and emphasis on marketing practices. The passage of power from sellers to buyers in the digital economy has given rise to the phenomenon of *reverse marketing,* where the customers call the shots.

Reverse Product Design

An increasing number of sites allow customers to design and configure their own products. Customers today can design their own computers (e.g., Dell or Gateway), jeans (e.g., ic3d.com or levi.com), and makeup (e.g., reflect.com). Tomorrow, they may be able to design their own shoes, cars, and even homes.

Reverse Pricing

The Internet allows consumers to move from being price takers to price makers. At Priceline.com, customers propose a price for specific items such as air travel, hotel rooms, mortgages, and automobiles. In searching for an automobile, a Priceline buyer specifies the price, model, options, pickup date, and distance they are willing to drive to complete the sale. Buyers provide their own financing and their guarantee with a $200 security deposit charged to their credit card. Priceline removes contact information from the offer and faxes it to all relevant dealers. Priceline makes its money on completed deals only. Buyers pay $25; dealers pay $75. Priceline plans to offer financing and insurance next, allowing consumers to shop using a similar price-quote model.

Reverse Advertising

Marketers have traditionally pushed their advertising at consumers, but the old broadcast model of advertising is increasingly being replaced by *narrowcasting*. In narrowcasting, a company uses direct mail or telemarketing to identify potential customers with a high probability of being interested in a particular product or service. In the future, buyers will take the initiative in determining which ads they want to see. They will need to give a company their permission before it can send them an ad. This is already particularly effective with e-mail, whereby customers can subscribe or unsubscribe to receiving e-mailed advertisements.

Pointcasting is a service that allows customers to click on ads that interest them. With pointcasting, advertising is customer initiated and pulled by customers. At their request, Amazon.com, for example, sends customers an e-mail message every time new books, CDs, and videos come out on subjects for which those customers have registered their interest. Amazon also uses the information in its database to customize the banner advertisements on its Web site.[16]

Reverse Promotions

Customers now can solicit coupons and promotions through marketing intermediaries such as Netcentives and mySimon.com. They can also request specific offers through marketing intermediaries such as MyPoints.com, FreeRide.com, and Internet service providers. They can request free samples of new products from FreeSamples.com. These intermediaries relay consumer requests to companies without necessarily divulging personal information.

Reverse Distribution Channels

The number of distribution channels for making offerings available and deliverable to customers is mushrooming. Many common products are available in grocery stores, drugstores, gas stations, and vending machines; they can even be delivered to the home by Peapod.com.

Digitized products, such as music, books, software, and film, can now be downloaded. Instead of traveling to a store to view clothing, customers view clothing in their own homes on the Internet (e.g., gap.com or landsend.com). The showroom comes to the customer instead of the customer going to the showroom. This suggests that companies must develop and manage more channels, which will complicate pricing and even require modifying offerings for the various channels.

Reverse Segmentation

The Internet allows the customer to inform companies of his or her likes, dislikes, and personal characteristics by answering a questionnaire. The information can be used by the company to construct customer segments. The company can then develop appropriate offerings for the different segments.[17]

Marketers can respond to reverse marketing by paying attention to the customer's four Cs: enhanced customer value, lower costs, improved convenience, and better communication. They need to explore the customer's cognitive space, assess the company's competency space, and capture the collaborators' resource space. We now turn to these issues.

EXPLORING THE CUSTOMER'S COGNITIVE SPACE

Customers' needs are of two types—*existing needs* and *latent needs*. Existing needs are those that customers currently have and can express. Latent needs are those that customers cannot express or do not believe can be satisfied. It often takes a company such as Sony to identify a latent need (portable music) and create a product solution (the Walkman).[18]

.ding to Kazuaki Ushikubo, customers' needs can be de-
in terms of a structure of elements that change as individuals
different contexts or move through different life-cycle stages.
Ushikubo recognizes two major social factors that drive human
wants: "chaos and order" and "outer and inner direction." The two
dimensions provide a framework for positioning four basic wants:
change, participation, freedom, and stability. These wants constitute
the person's "cognitive space." Ushikubo incorporates twelve factors
from Murray's list of human wants into the four quadrants (see figure
2-1). These basic wants suggest the different lifestyles described in
table 2-2.[19]

FIGURE 2-1   The Customer's Cognitive Space

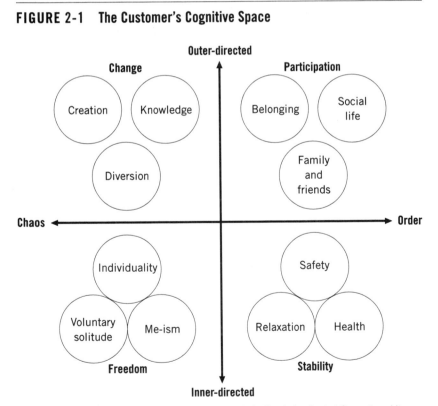

Source: Kazuaki Ushikubo, "A Method of Structure Analysis for Developing Product Concepts and Its
Applications," *European Research* 14, no. 4 (1986): 174–175.

TABLE 2-2   The Customer's Cognitive Subspace and Wants Factors

Subspace	Wants Factors	Meaning
Change	Diversion	I want to change my lifestyle occasionally
	Knowledge	I want to know more
	Creation	I want to do something to enhance myself
Participation	Family and friends	I want to have a pleasant time with my family and friends
	Belonging	I want to be like others
	Social life	I want to keep company with many different people
Freedom	Me-ism	I want to live as I like regardless of others
	Individuality	I want to be distinctive from others
	Voluntary solitude	I want to have my own world, apart from others
Stability	Relaxation	I want to relax and take a rest
	Safety	I want to keep myself safe
	Health	I want to be healthy in mind and body

Source: Kazuaki Ushikubo, "A Method of Structure Analysis for Developing Product Concepts and Its Applications," *European Research* 14, no. 4 (1986): 174–175.

The customer's cognitive space provides many business opportunities for marketers. It guides them to uncover latent demand opportunities. A personalized Web site, for example, can be created to serve the "me-ism" of the freedom subspace. Edutainment is developed to serve the "knowledge" and "relaxation" wants of change and stability subspaces.

Marketers, however, have to ensure that any latent demand idea would create real customer benefits. We discuss crafting customer benefits in chapter 3.

ASSESSING THE COMPANY'S COMPETENCY SPACE

Marketers must factor in the company's competency space in assessing market opportunities. Competency space can be described in terms of *competency breadth*—broad versus focused scope of business—and *competency depth*—physical versus knowledge-based capabilities.

Competency Breadth

Today's companies are eager to define their core competencies and then to outsource other activities that can be performed better and cheaper by other suppliers. Many companies are outsourcing their asset-intensive activities and focusing on their core competencies in one of the following three types of businesses.

Infrastructure business. An *infrastructure business* involves managing the high-volume, repetitive operations at the heart of manufacturing, warehousing, logistics, and communications. Examples include Oracle in database software, Cisco in Internet routers, America Online in providing Internet service, and FedEx in logistics service. FedEx, in turn, allies with many companies to provide warehousing, picking, packing, and delivery as a fully integrated part of the supply chain. Another example is the GE Trading Process Network. Companies use this facility to request quotations from participating Internet suppliers and then negotiate on the Internet to close the contracts.[20]

Product innovation and commercialization business. A *product innovation and commercialization business* engages in creating promising new ideas, products, and services and laying plans for their commercialization.[21] Examples include Sony in new electronic products, Liz Claiborne in women's apparel and accessories, Intel in microprocessors, and Disney in new entertainment.

Customer relationships business. A *customer relationships business* excels in building and managing strong brands and building and growing strong relationships with customers.[22] Examples include Amazon in retail selling and Charles Schwab in financial planning.

A retail bank, for example, could engage in one, two, or three businesses, depending on its desired competency breadth. A *product formulator business* will focus on developing products such as mortgages, savings accounts, and credit cards. A *customer intermediaries business* will capitalize on superior customer knowledge and efficient delivery channels. And an *outsource or syndicate business* will handle support functions such as communication infrastructure, risk economics, processing centers, and debt collection.[23]

Some companies fuse two or three businesses. Gateway's success is attributed to its innovation strength and customer relations, while it outsources the manufacturing job to others.

Competency Depth

In the digital economy, companies must decide whether they want to become knowledge-based companies or physical-based companies and then focus their strategies accordingly.

Knowledge-based companies will consider outsourcing or syndicating many of their capital-intensive processes, freeing up capital to focus on the parts of their business that differentiate the company. Knowledge-based companies will focus on building their brand(s), capitalizing on the customer relationship, and creating and upgrading their knowledge-based core competencies. They will rely on the Internet to get close to their customers, use data collection and data mining to develop unique customer offerings, outsource or syndicate nonstrategic parts of their business, and manage relationships with physical-based business partners.

In contrast, *physical-based companies* will orient their strategies, processes, systems, and organizations to become the best providers of raw materials and supplies to knowledge-based companies. They will differentiate themselves in the marketplace by providing product and service value to knowledge-based companies, managing capital (plants and equipment) effectively, and implementing efficient best practices. Traditional brick-and-mortar companies are oriented toward physical-based strategies.

In the digital economy, existing businesses will have to decide whether to remain physical-based, become knowledge-based, or split into some combination of the two.[24] We explore this in chapter 9.

CAPTURING COLLABORATORS' RESOURCE SPACE

The digital economy exhibits a spirit of exploration, learning, openness to change, and mutual support. To create new markets, companies may need to draw on resources from collaborators. Rather than doing too much on their own, companies will build collaborative networks. For example, iVillage asks American Baby to provide content to enrich its Web site instead of developing its own information on child-rearing issues. Rather than trying to attract sporting-goods buyers directly, Fogdog Sports joined with America Online to secure exposure within key departments of Shop@AOL; this enabled the start-up to leverage the substantial traffic that AOL had already aggregated.[25] Many companies have engaged in the codependent cycles of constant improvement and coevolution with their partners. Such partnerships take two forms—horizontal and vertical.

Horizontal partnerships. New economy companies define their core competencies and choose the best partners to exploit the related market opportunities. In the B2C market, Amazon and Dell, for example, announced in the spring of 1999 plans to encourage cross-marketing of their products by referring traffic to each other's sites.[26] In the B2B market, MetalSite consists of several steel companies that have formed a *horizontal partnership* to offer an online auction to dispose of excess inventory.

Direct collaborative networks among competitors, however, are more the exception than the rule. *Indirect collaboration* through a joint venture or third parties is more frequent. Airlines and railroads have already assigned third parties to manage duplicate inventories and assets held by competitors in the same locations. Instead of each airline with Airbus aircraft maintaining its own inventory of replacement parts at its major airports, a third-party inventory provider keeps a single stock at the same locations with much lower costs.[27]

Vertical partnerships. Amazon offers an "affiliate" program through which each collaborator can install a link to Amazon on their Web site and get a commission for any Amazon books that are purchased by customers who clicked through that link. Readers interested in cooking, for example, can browse the online cookbook store at StarChefs, a site for gourmets, click on a book to buy, and immediately get sent to Amazon.com to place the order. StarChefs then earns a referral fee of up to 15 percent.[28] To date, Amazon has established more than 350,000 affiliate links with its collaborators.

Ultimately, a company hopes to create and maintain the lifetime value stream emanating from the company, customers, collaborators, and community. The company needs to ensure its partners of a desirable future. Companies should enter each alliance with clear strategic objectives and understand how their partners' objectives will affect their success. Successful companies view each alliance as an access point to their partners' broad capabilities. We discuss this topic further in chapter 3.

BUILDING THE ENABLING ENVIRONMENT
FOR MARKET RENEWAL

Companies may gain market renewal ideas from four generic business channels, namely consumer-to-business (C2B), business-to-consumer (B2C), business-to-business (B2B), and consumer-to-consumer (C2C). A company can use its C2B channel to gain "outside-in" creative ideas from customer feedback. This C2B channel is particularly important because a larger proportion of original ideas comes from consumers than from within the company.[29] Call centers and company e-mail sites are effective customer interfaces, allowing the company not only to listen to but also to engage in a dialogue with the customer. The company can use its B2C channel to launch or test "inside-out" creative ideas and offerings to customers, communities, and collaborators. It can use its B2B channels to exchange "inside-in" ideas, innovations, and intelligence with its collaborators and employees. Finally, the company can use the C2C channel to access the "outside-out" innovative ideas, feedback, and comments from the interactive communities. These four channels can provide a wealth of market intelligence and ideas.

Today's companies are racing to acquire capabilities to design and deliver high-level value streams. An active partnership between companies and their customers, collaborators, and communities will help companies maximize company-delivered value and reduce company-delivered costs, as well as help companies respond faster to emerging opportunities.

QUESTIONS TO PONDER

- How much influence does your marketing department have over the other departments to persuade them to become customer-centered?

- What opportunities can marketers draw from the company-driven, customer-driven, collaborator-driven, and community-driven value streams?

- How far is your company willing to go in customizing its products and services for individual customers? Should it go further?

- Should your company still work through function-driven departments, or should it organize interdepartmental teams that manage key processes?

- What is your company doing to enter into and use the new marketspace? What other initiatives should your company take?

- How can your B2C marketers use the customer's cognitive space shown in figure 2-1?

- How can your company link its competency gaps with the resource space available from current and potential collaborators?

Part Two

CREATING COMPETITIVE PLATFORMS

THREE

Identifying
Market Opportunities

To exploit market opportunities, marketers need to complete three tasks: (1) craft the customers' benefits based on the changes in the consumers' cognitive space, (2) realign the company's business domain based on its competency space, and (3) expand the company's pool of business partners based on its collaborators' resource space. Following this, the company needs to integrate these activities with the right governance framework.

CRAFTING THE CUSTOMERS' BENEFITS

Every customer today is inundated with thousands of product and service offers. Yet each customer's cognitive and financial capacity is limited. What customers really care about are their own needs and how to fulfill them. To identify a consumer's needs, marketers must understand his *choice context:* what the customer thinks about, wants, does, and worries about. Marketers must also observe whom customers are admiring, whom they are interacting with, and who influences them.

Three Major Shifts in Customer Benefits

Shifting the focus from the company's product attributes to the customer's contextual experience yields new insights and ideas. Customer benefits are now being defined along three dimensions:

1. From output-based offerings to outcome- and input-based offerings

2. From product performance to customer experiences

3. From mass-market offerings to customized market offerings

From output-based offerings to outcome- and input-based offerings. In the digital economy, marketers can choose between two market offering strategies—outcome-based and input-based.

Outcome-based offerings. Marketers attempt to minimize customer defection by providing *outcome-* or *solution-based offerings.* Consider the health area. Most companies emphasize disease management. But a new marketspace for health promotion is emerging in which health care providers replace the current fee-for-service system with a system that bases fees on making or keeping individuals well. The next step is a marketspace that would focus on total well-being and life-extension management.

Every supplier must define the outcome its customers seek. Consumers want good taste and nutrition, not foodstuffs; healthy teeth, not toothpaste; entertainment, not CDs; clean clothes, not laundry products; the ability to communicate, not communications equipment. In redefining their business, automakers should offer a mobility service that would combine the vehicle purchase with finance, insurance, leasing, and roadside repair. Instead of offering loans, a bank should offer lifelong-events cash management. Computer service companies should aim to transform low-productivity client businesses into high-productivity businesses.

Companies like FedEx create value not just for their customers but also for their customers' customers. By offering reliable package delivery, FedEx provides value to the receiver of the package (the indirect customer) as well as to the sender of the package (the direct customer).[1]

In the insurance business, current policy carriers insure their policyholders to receive a payment in the event of a loss. But Rand Merchant Bank in South Africa offers "outsurance" instead of "insurance"; it pays customers for *not* claiming, and it doesn't hike their premiums if they do submit claims. Aegon, an insurance company in the Netherlands, rewards customers who keep fit and stay healthy to a certain age. And the Swedish insurance company Skandia has launched "competence insurance," by which an individual builds up savings to pay for educational experiences to maintain his competence in case of job changes.[2]

Input-based offerings. Market value can also be delivered by *input-based offerings*, in which the customer plays a major role in designing and building the product or service. In developing input-based offerings, marketers ask their customers, "What capabilities do you want?" The company then acts as a building-block provider and order facilitator.

The Japanese retailer Muji, for example, provides basic, unornamented, and functional unbranded products from which people can build their own lifestyles. "As society is becoming more uniform," says Muji's president, Ariga Kaoru, "young people will build lifestyles on their own values." Muji encourages people to move away from fashion brands and search for simplicity instead.[3] Other examples of input-based offerings include The Home Depot's do-it-yourself repair and remodeling projects and Gap.com's clothing design.

From product performance to customer experiences. Many market offerings are becoming more similar because of the increasing capability
of companies to copy one another. As Paul Goldberger, chief cultural
correspondent of the *New York Times,* said about product design,
"While everything may be better, it is also increasingly the same."[4]
Consequently, customers now find themselves choosing among experiential themes rather than among product features.

Today, companies win their customers by allowing them to manage their own experience. Instead of focusing on how the market
offering performs, companies are looking at how the individual customer performs while using the market offering. Many theme restaurants—Hard Rock Café and Dive!, for instance—offer foods as a prop
for "eatertainment." Stores such as FAO Schwarz, Jordan's Furniture,
and Niketown are reorienting their businesses toward "shoppertain-
ment" or "entertailing" by drawing consumers into fun activities and
promotional events.

Other examples include the Ritz-Carlton lodging experience, the
Hertz car-renting experience, the Select Comfort sleeping experience,
the Lutron lighting experience, and the Peapod grocery shopping
experience.[5] Even input-based offerings, like those of Intel, can aim to
deliver an experience, as stated by Intel chairman Andrew Grove: "We
need to look at our business as more than simply the building and
selling of personal computers. Our business is the delivery of information and lifelike interactive experiences."[6]

From mass-market offerings to customized market offerings. In the industrial age, companies delivered highly standardized mass-produced
offerings. Today, digitization allows real customization. Customers
can specify the features they want in a product, service, or experience.
Levi's customers can custom-size their jeans; Dell's customers can
customize their computers. Internet music vendors offer customized
CDs by allowing customers to specify only the tracks they want. Some

sites even have a "Call Me" button that, when clicked, draws an immediate phone call from the company to respond to an individual customer's need.[7] These companies come much closer to satisfying individual needs than do mass marketers.

REALIGNING THE COMPANY'S BUSINESS DOMAIN

The shift toward maximizing customers' contextual experiences requires marketers to realign their company's business domain. Their
companies will need new capabilities and possibly new collaborators.
Banks, for example, will need to be available to customers on a twenty-
four-hour basis, not the traditional 9 A.M. to 5 P.M. hours. They will
have to put ATMs in more locations and offer online banking in order
to provide the experience that their retail customers expect.

Global forces and trends also necessitate changes in a company's
business domain. The global trend toward deregulation, for example,
has led to a rise in companies other than banks offering a wide range
of financial services. Automaker Volkswagen is now one of the largest
non-bank providers of financial services in Europe. Starting by serving customers with car loans, it has expanded its financial services to
include mortgage loans and many savings instruments.[8]

Other macro-level trends—globalization, alliance building, outsourcing, and syndication—also call for business realignment. "Microsoft already has links with businesses that bring it into direct competition with major media groups such as Time Warner and News
Corporation. It owns more than 10% of Comcast, one of America's
largest cable companies, and it has a joint venture with the Disney
Corporation to develop material for the Internet."[9]

Digital technology is one of the major forces shaping competitive dynamics. On the one hand, it allows new companies such as
Travelocity.com, Amazon.com, and E*TRADE to bypass traditional

middlemen and sell direct. On the other hand, it allows new middlemen to emerge on the Internet. For example, information middlemen (e.g., comparenet.com) present and compare the features and prices of all available brands supplied by various Internet merchants. Their effect is to lower the seller's prices, increase the customer's product and pricing knowledge, and earn profits for middlemen in the process.

To cope with the competitive threats, traditional middlemen have only two recourses: reinvent themselves or disappear. They can survive by assuming the role of logistics service providers, information service providers, or intermediaries that offer an attractive range of products and services. Alternatively, with digital technology, they can survive through forward integration. Ingram, a leading U.S. computer wholesaler, extended its business into e-direct sales by starting Buycomp.com. Following its success, Ingram extended its market to other types of goods and changed its sales site's name to Buy.com.

Every company should take three steps to realign its business: (1) (re)define its business concept, (2) (re)shape its business scope, and (3) (re)position its brand identity.

(Re)defining the Company's Business Concept

In a very dynamic and competitive environment, a company needs a focused strategy. The focus, however, should be on a "big idea" rather than on a product category, a certain market segment, or a specific core competency.

Today's successful companies do not view themselves as selling products or services as much as exploring, creating, and delivering customer value. Their sense of purpose captures the imaginations of their customers, collaborators, and employees. Customers, for example, don't consider IKEA to be a furniture maker but a company standing for the bigger idea of "a better everyday life for the many."

Other companies also operate with a "big idea":

• Disney is in the "making people happy" business.

• Saturn is beyond cars; it is about "harmony."

• Sony and Bang & Olufsen are more than consumer electronics companies: Sony is about "miniature perfection," and Bang & Olufsen is about "poetry."

• Amazon is about "completeness," as illustrated by the arrow on its logo stretching from the *a* to the *z* of *amazon* and reflecting the idea that people can get anything from Amazon.

• Starbucks provides a place where people feel at home as they drink coffee, chat, and read the papers; it is more about "sociability" than about coffee.

• Southwest Airlines projects a spirit where "flying is fun."

• Cisco, a manufacturer of networks equipment, believes in an "outside-in" way of running its business; it is about giving customers an extraordinary degree of power over its corporate and business strategies.

Many companies in the digital economy have transformed themselves into navigators or agents that enable people to explore the market and find the best market offerings to serve their needs.

(Re)shaping the Company's Business Scope

To turn customer benefits into a real business opportunity, a company may have to enlarge or otherwise adjust the scope of its business. Supermarkets have done so by adding gasoline stations and Web-based grocery ordering and delivery services.[10] Here are additional examples:

- Barclays Group has become the owner of seventeen online malls and has changed its name to Barclays Square to reflect its new business domain.

- The former British Gas has changed its name to BG and turned itself into a major seller of energy-saving products on the Web.

- British Telecom makes three times as much money from the new services it provides over its network as it does from the network itself.

- Some media companies, such as QVC, are also retail operations; others, such as Reuters and Bloomberg, have diversified into financial services businesses.

- Some energy companies, such as Shell, Mobil, and BP, are entering retailing; others, such as Energis, have spawned telecommunications companies.[11]

- 1-800-FLOWERS defines its business as "serving its customers' gift-giving needs" rather than as selling flowers.[12]

- Travelocity is extending its role of selling airline tickets to providing a range of travel-related services.[13]

- U.K. retailer Boots the Chemist offers a variety of health products, including health insurance, under the Boots brand.[14]

Many not-for-profit organizations are also undertaking the business-reshaping process. The British Council, a government agency promoting British culture around the world, runs money-making English schools. It plays the role of a business and an educational charity simultaneously.[15]

Two basic questions should be asked about business reshaping: "What is the company's current scope of businesses?" and "What should be the company's scope of businesses, given the redefined business concept?" Toshifumi Suzuki, former president of Seven-Eleven Japan, saw this distinction and turned his retail business into an information business:

> *[Suzuki] used information technology to drive convenience, quality, service and customer needs by ensuring that shelves were replenished several times a day in response to orders from individual store managers. He also established a large field counselor organization to train store operators not only how to capture customer and sales information but how to exploit this information.*[16]

As more companies gradually shift their operations from a marketplace with a physical value chain to a marketspace with a virtual value chain, they need to do serious rethinking about the scope of their business.

(Re)positioning the Company's Brand Identity

To communicate effectively with customers and collaborators, marketers must ensure that the company's brand identity reflects its smart business concept(s) and reshaped business scope. Many leading industrial age companies were inside-out organizations—focused on themselves rather than on their customers. In the digital economy, however, companies are competing to be the one with the brilliant idea, concept, or theme. Many strong brands today are outside-in— unique and highly personal:[17]

- Microsoft's "Where do you want to go today?" stands for "ubiquity."

- Apple's "The power to be your best" and "Think Different" stand for "differences."

- Nike's "Just Do It" and "I Can" stand for "winning."

The company may even choose a brand name to signify its offering, such as CarPoint (automobile sales and financing) and Home-Advisor (real estate).[18]

EXPANDING THE BUSINESS PARTNER SPACE

Tackling market opportunities requires not only understanding customer trends and realigning the company's business domain but also attracting needed resources to capitalize on the opportunity. Many of these resources must come from business partners.

Traditional companies had linked with one another in a simple, linear chain, progressing from raw-material processors to manufacturers to distributors to retailers. The *collaborative network* replaces the linear chain as the digital economy's operating model. Companies should seek to capture the most valuable niches in collaborative networks—which turn out to be niches that maximize the number and strength of their ties with other companies as well as with their customers. However, these ties are subject to changes, so even the most successful businesses may constantly have to reevaluate and revise them.

A company can link with its business partners in two main ways—through outsourcing and syndication.

Linking through Outsourcing

Companies should focus on their core competencies and outsource other activities to firms that can provide superior performance and/or lower costs. Here are some possibilities highlighted by David Edelman and Dieter Heuskel:[19]

- *Outsourcing innovation or technology.* A company with superior innovation and design capabilities could keep them in-house and may even decide to sell or license them on the open market. Procter & Gamble, for example, developed a process for adding calcium to citrus juices, but instead of using it exclusively for its own brand, P&G licenses the process to other fruit juice companies. On the other hand, if a company could obtain useful technology from outside firms, it would make sense to do so.

- *Outsourcing manufacturing.* If a company has excellent production capabilities but lacks brand strength, opportunities abound for it to become a supplier of private-label merchandise. Conversely, if a company wants to specialize in brand ownership rather than physical asset ownership, it will need to assemble a network of suppliers. It is imperative that companies consider any cost and technology advantages they may lose in outsourcing their manufacturing.

- *Outsourcing or leveraging distribution.* A company with efficient delivery capabilities could do its own distribution and possibly even sell distribution services to others. By contrast, if a company's in-house delivery capabilities are deficient, it should consider engaging an outside distributor. Companies should recognize, however, that using a distributor might decrease the company's ability to achieve advantage through customized service.

Linking through Syndicating

A company can secure information or a service from a *syndicator,* a company that sells content to a large number of parties at a small incremental cost. Reuters acts as a syndicator in that it gathers news from a wide variety of sources and sells this news to a great number of companies, such as E*TRADE. E*TRADE does not want to produce its own content. Instead it "rents" content from many syndicators, including Reuters for financial news, BigCharts.com for stock charts, and Bridge Information Systems for stock quotes. These syndicators themselves normally do not originate the content but rather package it for distributors, including E*TRADE. If E*TRADE were to develop some original content, it might decide to syndicate that material to other financial companies.[20]

Besides information content, commercial processes can also be syndicated. Syndicators may offer a credit-scoring algorithm, a shopping-cart ordering and payment system, or a logistics algorithm. An Internet start-up can then "rent" these business processes without having to create the software itself.

In sum, both outsourcing and syndication provide several benefits:

- They can improve the company's competitive position and hence its profitability.

- They enable companies to focus on their core competencies and hire other companies to handle the remaining activities in a complete end-to-end service.

- They reduce the required investment in capability and infra-structure.

- They increase organizational flexibility to meet rapidly changing economic conditions and technology advances.

Maintaining outsourcing and syndication relationships, however, requires high levels of trust and mutual benefit.

DEVELOPING A CORPORATE GOVERNANCE FRAMEWORK

In spite of rapidly changing market dynamics, companies must maintain strategic coherence through connectivity and interactivity with their customers and collaborative networks. Companies need a proper *corporate governance framework* to integrate and organize customer benefits, business partner arrangements, and business scope.

Governance is the glue that binds the relationship between the company and its stakeholders. It goes far beyond the rules and regulations that define corporate boundaries as a legal entity. Amir Hartman, John Sifonis, and John Kador argue that a governance charter should encourage teamwork, set explicit and measurable goals, delegate authority and responsibility, and ensure accountability and consistency in decision making throughout the organization.[21]

Governance deals with some of the toughest questions that companies face today, such as:

- Should the company spin off a separate organization for its Internet activities or integrate these efforts into its existing structure?

- How much of a company's investment should go to maintaining the existing business and how much should go to developing new business? Does the company have effective methods for assessing and selecting business initiatives and for allocating resources?

- Who has decision-making authority in the company's new businesses? How can management make sure that the new businesses operate consistently with the existing businesses?

A company must be able to maintain the integrity of its strategy in the face of changing conditions and yet be able to shift appropriately in response to new conditions. The need is to strike a balance between *alignment* and *adaptability*. While alignment defines a strategy, adaptability allows companies to change direction in midstream. Alignment will keep the company focused and moving toward a shared goal with its partners. Each partner takes on well-defined roles and responsibilities. Performance scorecards are kept and measured continually. Accountability for results is stressed and backed by sanctions and rewards.

Adaptability requires a company periodically to reexamine and test its current assumptions, such as "We sell through dealers, we don't sell to our customers directly"; "We can't cooperate with company X because we compete with company X"; and "Employees can't be trusted so we have to monitor their profitability and get after them when they're lax."[22] Some of these assumptions may have to be changed. The company may have to reorient the organization and its partners in response to new opportunities or threats. It needs to exchange its viewpoints with its partners. The company and its partners may singly or jointly conduct experiments and implement new ideas. Room must be made for modifying institutional systems and relationships in light of changing markets and technology.[23]

QUESTIONS TO PONDER

- Does your company define its benefits by outputs (i.e., products and services) or by outcomes?

- Has your company gone far enough in customizing its offerings for individual customers? If not, why?

- What are your company's core competencies? What activities might your company outsource or syndicate to others?

- Does your company's governance framework provide enough latitude for adaptability to changing conditions?

FOUR

Designing Winning Market Offerings

The first set of basic building blocks—cognitive space, competency space, customer benefits, and business domain—gives marketers strategic insight for managing the market offerings platform (see figure 4-1).

We start by elaborating the variety of possible market offerings. Then we examine two generic market offering strategies—broadening the customer benefits (through choice maps) and deepening the customer benefits (through choice boards). Finally, we examine how marketers craft the value proposition to strengthen these market-offering strategies.

ELABORATING THE VARIETY OF POSSIBLE MARKET OFFERINGS

Companies today have countless opportunities to provide different market offerings.[1] Such offerings can be classified as follows:

FIGURE 4-1   The Market Offering Platform

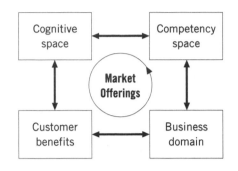

- Digital and physical offerings

- Intangible and tangible offerings

- Features and intelligence offerings

- Container and content offerings

Digital and Physical Offerings

Digital offerings are mostly information-related goods and services, such as financial services, news services, entertainment and multimedia products, and software distribution services. These products are, by nature, difficult to value but easy to imitate. Yet the digital world shows no mercy for imitators. Merely copying Dell Computer or Amazon.com is a losing proposition.

The Internet has spawned innovative digital products such as online advertising, online gaming, chat rooms, search engines, and certification services. To market these digital offerings, companies pursue several programs such as introducing different versions (versioning), customizing, and bundling.

Digital technologies have significantly reconfigured the functionality of many *physical offerings*. Digital cameras, for instance, have succeeded 35-millimeter cameras. Digital cameras perform new functions, such as allowing users to print their own images, send them to others by e-mail, put them on the Internet, and show them on the television screen.[2]

United Parcel Service uses the Internet to position itself as not only a physical package deliverer but also an information deliverer. Its Document Exchange service helps businesses transmit documents cheaply and securely over the Internet, with the same benefits that it offers for physical packages (e.g., package tracking and delivery confirmation). The Internet also enables UPS to customize logistics for its customers (e.g., ensuring that parts from different countries arrive when and where they are needed).

Intangible and Tangible Offerings

For every type of market offering there is a different mix of intangible actions and tangible enablers. Craig Terrill and Arthur Middlebrooks categorize offerings into four groups, based on who or what receives the offering: people's minds (e.g., consulting and information services), people's bodies (e.g., restaurants and passenger transportation), physical assets (e.g., overnight mail services and car repair), and intangible assets (e.g., insurance and banking).[3] In most cases, customers care little about the tangible items that help deliver the promised experience; instead, they care about the outcome or experience itself. Thus, many companies now focus on differentiating the intangible actions that create the desired customer experience.

Features and Intelligence Offerings

Technology today is embedded in and around products to make them "smarter." The financial value of a car's smart electronics now exceeds the value of its steel body. Chips are embedded in many electronic home appliances such as microwave ovens and stereos, just as they have become standard components of elevators and vending machines. Schlumberger and Swatch have launched a new contact-less, electronic-ticketing watch, called *Swatch Access,* which packs a smart-card payment system for public transit fares. In the B2B market, many companies use the Internet to deliver value by replacing, upgrading, or eliminating routine manual processes.

Container and Content Offerings

Products are either predominantly *containers,* machines such as movie projectors or printers, or *content,* value-added intelligence such as videos and software. Containers generally have little value unless content is added to them. Movie projectors are useless without movies to project; printers are useless without documents to print.

Many companies specialize in either the container or the content business. But digital technologies are blurring the distinction between containers and content. A content company may decide to add containers, and a container company might decide to add content. Companies may not have to exit one space to engage in the other; they can often reap benefits from both.

Although the container can be a tangible, such as a PC or a microchip, its most intrinsic value may be as an intangible, such as "architecture, an application, a channel, an infrastructure, or a platform."[4]

DESIGNING MARKET OFFERINGS

Companies can design market offerings in two ways. Marketers can broaden customer value by creating or facilitating the customers' contextual experience. Alternately, marketers can deepen value to the customer by individualizing the market offerings to match the individual customer's contextual experience. We use the concepts of a choice map and a choice board to describe the two approaches.

DEVELOPING A CHOICE MAP

A *choice map* provides a set of choices from which individual customers can select to meet their needs in a specific context or for a specific period of time. Marketers can develop a choice map by taking these three steps: (1) assess the customer consumption chain, (2) understand the customer learning experience, and (3) develop the contextual offerings based on the customer consumption chain and learning experience.

Assessing the Customer Consumption Chain

Understanding the customer's life context is the key to preparing a differentiated market offering. Marketers should ask consumers to chart their steps in selecting, acquiring, using, and disposing of an offering. With this information, marketers can consider whether the company can introduce some new value or benefits to each step in the consumption chain.

Here is a sample set of questions for mapping the consumption chain:[5]

• How do people become aware of their need for the offering?

• How do they locate the offering?

• How do they make their final purchasing decisions?

• How do they order and purchase the offering?

• How is the offering delivered?

- What happens when the offering is delivered?

- How is the offering installed?

- How is the offering paid for?

- How is the offering stored?

- How is the offering moved around?

- What is the customer really using the offering to do?

- What do customers need help with when they use the offering?

- What is the policy toward returns or exchanges?

- How is the offering repaired or serviced?

- How is the offering disposed of?

Sandra Vandermerwe developed a similar idea, which she calls mapping the "customer activity cycle."[6] The consumption chain (or customer activity cycle) helps companies view the larger value chain. For example, the simple act of washing clothes in a washing machine has been facilitated by the value chains that the washing machine maker, the detergent manufacturer, the clothing manufacturer, the electricity supplier, and the water supplier have created.[7] Identifying each activity in the value chain helps marketers to envision new ways of linking these value chains to serve customers better.

Mohanbir Sawhney observed that companies think in terms of products and services, while consumers think in terms of activities. Activities that are rationally linked in the cognitive realm are usually provided by multiple providers in the market. Sawhney coined the term *metamarkets* for such cognitively linked actions performed by customers to fulfill a specific set of needs.[8] Examples of metamarkets include buying a car (purchasing, financing, insuring, and accessorizing the car), buying a new home (involving contracting the services of electricians, plumbers, and carpenters), and planning a wedding (involving choosing flowers, wedding gowns, and invitations).

The customer consumption chain, customer activity cycle, and metamarket concepts guide marketers in understanding the choice context of individual customers. In many cases, product performance may have less impact on perceived performance than does the stream of related activities. Consider the bookstore business. Barnes & Noble and Borders bookstores expanded the customer experience in a bookstore to include chairs and tables, coffee and pastry bars, book clubs, and author events and performances. They focused on the customer chain of activity such as browsing books, meeting friends, having coffee, and listening to speakers.[9]

SCA, the Swedish paper company, broadened its consumption view of the baby diaper business. SCA created the Web site www.libero.dk as a community for expectant and current parents. The site offers information from experts and peers on parenting, such as tips for choosing the right kind of diapers, lists of names, and so on. Users can purchase and sell children's gear for free and can create individual Web sites for their babies—including photos that friends and relatives around the world can access.[10]

Understanding the Consumer Learning Experience

To develop the choice map, a company needs to study the consumer learning experience. There are two kinds of consumer learning: process-based and content-based. *Process-based learning* refers to learning about the features of the offering and how to use it. For example, when finding out about a yellow pages Web site, people may want to learn how to search the address database and define the parameters and the scope of the search. Process-based learning determines a consumer's ability to use an offering—that is, its "usability."

Content-based learning refers to learning about the information residing in a market offering. In the yellow pages example, content-based learning includes finding out about the comprehensiveness of the listings, the depth and breadth of information about each business, and the accuracy of that information. Content-based learning determines a consumer's evaluation of how effective an offering is— that is, its "usefulness."[11]

Marketers should design learning experiences to match the customer's choice context, enabling consumers to maximize their return on their learning investment.

Developing the Contextual Offerings

By starting with customer goals and contexts and then working backwards, companies can find new ways of doing things. Kodak's online PhotoNet service, for example, has a unique value proposition for its customers: They can obtain digital versions of their photographs on a personal Kodak page when they develop their film at a Kodak store.[12]

Vandermerwe provides additional examples of contextual offerings:[13]

- Mondex's new ways for customers to pay for their small-ticket purchases by using a smart card

- Mercedes's new ways for customers to move about by having several cars at their disposal

- Peapod's new ways for customers to obtain their daily supplies by home delivery

- Direct Line's new ways for customers to cover and handle their auto risks by ordering auto insurance online

Separating form and function. Any market offering combines form with function. The form of a consulting service, for example, is the face-to-face meeting of consultant and client; the function of the consulting service is to identify issues, conduct diagnoses, and make recommendations. Separating the functionality of a value chain from its physical form creates enormous opportunities. Cisco, for example, has eliminated the need for the physical presence of engineers and test equipment by testing its components virtually and digitizing its quality assurance processes. Thus, Cisco found a way to change the form of delivering the function while saving money and shortening the delivery cycle.[14]

The same is true of Microsoft. When users have a problem with Windows, they make a phone call and interact with a technician who tells them how to reboot, select Start and then Run, and type in "msconfig." The technician then walks them through a sequence of steps, asking questions along the way. This form of solving the customer's problem is preferable to the alternative of shipping the computer back to the company.

Digitization enables companies to separate the functions from the traditional forms of their market offerings, creating new business opportunities in the process. The Borders bookstore chain, for example, is looking to combine digitization with customization to help it squeeze more value out of its brick-and-mortar retail operations. Borders acquired the digital book wholesaler Sprout, hoping to put together a system for printing books on demand inside its stores. Sprout's books were stored in digital form, and any book could be printed and bound at a customer's request. This way, Borders could reduce the cost of storing and shipping books, increase the number of available titles, and eliminate the risk of returns.[15]

The form of an offering usually follows its functions. In some cases, however, form conflicts with function. People who need to replace spark plugs in a Chevrolet Monza, for example, must remove the engine to get at them. And *Wired* magazine readers must maneuver their way around a difficult design to read the content they're after.

Bundled versus focused offerings. Few market offerings are pure and focused; most are bundled together. Banks bundle payment services, security of savings, the provision of account information, and other services. Auto dealerships bundle the sale of new cars, the purchase of secondhand ones, the provision of customer finance, and the delivery of repairs. Newspapers bundle news, opinion, features, classified advertising, and entertainment.

Digital technology allows companies and customers to unbundle as well as to bundle market offerings. For example, a customer can buy a particular song of his or her choice rather than an entire album, or an article or chapter from a book instead of the whole book.

A bundling approach typically involves cross subsidies. One customer's cross subsidy, however, is usually another's mispricing. Digital technology allows new, focused entrants to expose those cross subsidies and mispricing issues. Online new-car sales agencies, such as Microsoft's CarPoint, help unbundle an auto dealer's offerings. E-classifieds eliminate the cross subsidy to news. Financial services products exploit and then outcompete the cross subsidies inherent in retail banking.

Many businesses now have shifted some of their "service" to their customers. Banks, for example, have turned their customers into tellers through their ATMs; FedEx has turned its customers into shippers; gas stations have turned their customers into self-service gas pumpers; and the phone company has turned its customers into operators.

OFFERING A CHOICE BOARD

With a choice map, companies learn how customers go about solving a problem. With a choice board, companies can deepen the value of their offering to customers through customization, customerization, and collaboration.

A *choice board* is a virtual interactive system that enables individual customers to design their own products by choosing from a menu of attributes, components, prices, and delivery options. The customer's selections immediately send signals to the company's operational system, which initiates the process of procurement, assembly, and delivery.[16]

Choice boards have many benefits. They enable Weyerhaeuser's door division to design custom-made doors in fifteen minutes, rather than the usual month, by engaging in two-way interactions with suppliers. Premier Dell.com provides value to Dell's large corporate clients by allowing their central procurement departments to customize their own choice boards. Thus, customers within those corporations can choose exactly what they want while the companies can manage the choice set. Choice boards give individual customers the flexibility to customize products to suit their specific needs. And marketers can use choice boards to keep track of consumer preferences and hence better forecast demand.[17]

Not all choice boards are confined to the Internet. Dell and Gateway launched the first choice boards—real-time interactive ordering—over the telephone. Gateway enhances its phone and Internet choice board service with direct support at its wide network of Gateway Country stores. Thus, companies can assist customers with choice boards in a variety of contexts.[18]

We now turn to the roles that customization, customerization, and collaboration play in preparing market offerings.

Customization

The Internet allows companies to offer customized solutions in response to unique demands. The purest form of mass customization is *build-to-order* (BTO). Examples include transforming an ill patient into a healthy one; converting zoning approvals, blueprints, and construction materials into a building; and turning a vision into a product design. BTO shop activities are ad hoc, styled and scaled to a particular customer or project. Each customer or project involves a unique set of value-creating activities, so the shops are driven entirely by demand. In a medical practice, there is no "production" without a sick patient seeking treatment.[19] Well-designed BTO models can actually be cheaper than traditional mass-production models because they allow marketers to see the customer's actual order and they avoid the huge inventory costs in building to stock. The latter can be especially costly in industries with short product life cycles.

Companies can also achieve a certain level of customization through channel assembly and postponement. *Channel assembly* allows manufacturers to complete final product assembly at the reseller level or in the store. Sun Microsystems, for example, considers resellers an extension of its manufacturing value chain and trains them to perform final assembly of customer-configured systems on their own premises.[20] *Postponement* is a milder form of customization. It is a "tool of customizing the partially completed product close to the customer, where knowledge of actual demand is more accurate." Many companies have viewed postponement as the solution to the demand/supply imbalances in their businesses.[21]

There are three basic types of customization: adaptive, cosmetic, and transparent. In *adaptive customization,* the company gives the customer a standard offering with many options. For example, customers customize their Web access according to their individual needs. In the software business, BroadVision offers business-to-business personalization software that combines marketer-controlled customer behavior information with customer-specified preferences to create tailored commission structures, tailored pricing information, educational programs, profile-accelerated transactions, and activity reports.[22]

Cosmetic customization occurs when a company presents a generic product differently to different users. The *New York Times,* for example, requires free registration on its Web site. By storing a cookie (special text stored in a file created by the browser software) on a user's machine, the *Times* can link the users with their registration information. When users access the online newspaper, they are greeted by their name as part of the news page. Eventually, users will be able to specify the topics about which they want to receive news.[23]

In *transparent customization,* a company can make a unique offering to each customer without having to alert the customer. Staff at Ritz-Carlton hotels observe and record individual guest preferences and enter them into the company's database. When that guest arrives again, he or she is assigned a room with all preferences met—without even being asked.[24]

As product-based differentiation diminishes in importance and value, marketers are competing more by customizing their add-on services. In fact, mass customization is actually easier and cheaper in handling services than in making products.

Not all businesses can make profits from customization. According to Martha Rogers and Don Peppers, the combination of customer differences, customer values, and personalization enables companies to create customer advantage. Customization is unprofitable when the needs of customers are uniform and the lifetime value of customers is similar, as in the case of gasoline and table salt. Personalization and one-to-one marketing are most effective when there are high variations in customer needs and profit potential, as in professional services.[25]

Customization involves two risks. The first is that if it is easy to imitate, competitors will enter a vicious circle of increasing investments from which, ultimately, only consumers benefit. The second is that if the product is not designed carefully and the dissatisfied customer returns it, the company is then stuck with an idiosyncratic product that no other customer may want.[26]

Customerization

Customerization describes situations in which customers, rather than the company, take the lead in designing the offerings. Here are some examples:

- Supersonic Boom offers thousands of music tracks that users can download and use to create their own CDs.

- Dell Computer's online configuration tools allow customers to design their own computers.

- Mattel's My Design Barbie lets customers create their own dolls.

Customerization results in customer-led product design, value proposition, and positioning. The company offers a customerization platform to minimize customer defection and maximize customer satisfaction.

Collaboration

Collaboration occurs when a company and its customers actively conduct a dialogue and work together in co-customizing the offerings. Many companies use extranets to carry on a dialogue with their important suppliers and customers. These discussions can be concise or extended and can vary from simple surveys to videoconferences. Companies now use this feedback from their most valuable clients to customize their market offerings.[27]

Many B2B companies have actively used collaboration. Procter & Gamble, for example, has shortened its uploading time for shipments from 211 minutes to just 94 minutes by offering incentives to customers who agree to take dock delivery of shipments within two hours or less at least 80 percent of the time.[28]

Collaboration also takes place in specific functions, such as design and engineering or consulting. In some B2B relationships, the customer's and supplier's stock-management systems are tightly interconnected to minimize the working capital. For example, Procter & Gamble has agreed to use Wal-Mart's information system to take responsibility for stocking and managing Wal-Mart's inventory of P&G products.

CRAFTING THE RIGHT VALUE PROPOSITION

Marketers should ensure that the choice map and choice boards, derived from the customer's cognitive space and customer benefits, align with new business concepts, derived from the company's competency space and business domain. This strategic coherence is critical in crafting the right value proposition for persuading customers to purchase their company's market offerings.

Companies that pioneer a new business may or may not formulate the best value proposition, although they are in a better position to succeed than are later followers. Being first in the market provides access to the highest tier collaborators, the best talents, and the most valuable customers. First movers have a better chance of establishing their brands in an uncrowded market and hence to get a capitalization premium. Their goal, therefore, is to gain mind-share as soon as possible because only the mind-share leaders and monopolies will reap the benefits of network effects.

Marketers, however, should keep in mind that the Internet is still in its infancy. Late entrant companies, instead of imitating pioneers, should develop a value proposition for their market offerings primarily based on a big idea backed by innovative business concepts and excellent design.

Marketers should brand the idea behind their market offering as well as the offering itself. They need to communicate the value proposition in a vivid way. Southwest Airlines positions itself as a choice that is "cheaper and faster than driving"; Mandarin Oriental offers "moments of pleasure"; Bose claims that listening to its AM/FM radios is better than being at a concert hall; and Edmunds.com offers an "inventory of opinion" on cars and their ratings.

Companies can develop innovative value propositions for their offerings in a variety of ways. Southwest Airlines and easyJet aim to make air travel as accessible as bus travel. They have destroyed the myth that air travel is a luxury by combining the speed of flying with the convenience of frequent departures and the low cost of driving.

Some firms create a value proposition by featuring many related product lines, modeled on the department store or shopping mall idea. Amazon.com, for example, has extended its scope by selling CDs and setting up a drugstore, a toy store, a lawn and garden store, and so on; it is rapidly becoming a comprehensive online department store.[29]

Offering one-stop shopping for a product category and all related items is another innovative value proposition. Travelocity.com, for example, helps travelers find airline routes, the best fares, hotels, and related travel and destination information. Wal-Mart has positioned itself as a one-stop life-needs provider. Toys-R-Us is positioned as a one-stop toys and games provider. The Gap is positioned as a one-stop clothing-needs provider.[30]

Some companies accelerate the value-creating and -delivering processes by sensing and responding to customer needs faster than their competitors. Cemex, the Mexican cement producer, promises to deliver concrete faster than pizza: If a customer's order is more than ten minutes late, that customer gets a 20 percent discount. Cemex transformed its business by using extensive networking technology— Global Positioning System real-time location signals from every truck, powerful telecommunications throughout the company, and full delivery information available to drivers and dispatchers who have the authority to act on it.[31]

Here are additional examples of companies that are winning by responding faster:

- "Music on CDs is a very data-intensive medium. It used to take several hours to download a typical CD in native format. But MPEG Layer 3 audio compression technology (MP3) provides 12-to-1 data reduction without degradation of music quality. With it, a CD that once took four hours to download can now be downloaded in 20 minutes."[32]

- Plymouth Rock Assurance Corporation created Crash Busters to hasten the process of settling insurance claims in car accidents. Most insurance companies make payments to their clients only after obtaining estimates from auto body shops, getting appraisals from the adjuster, and processing paperwork. But a Crash Busters van, equipped with a computer, mobile phone, printer, and modem, reaches the scene of the accident with a claims appraiser who makes the necessary appraisals and reimburses the customer immediately.[33]

- Dell provides quick responses to customer problems. As soon as a customer calls for sales or service, the Dell representative can look up the exact configuration of the customer's machine and his complete purchase history, which helps the rep to diagnose the problem.

Some companies gain competitive advantage by increasing their level of local responsiveness. Amazon.com entered the European market with two new Web sites—amazon.co.uk (the United Kingdom) and amazon.de (Germany). As CEO Jeff Bezos pointed out, "We want to make it possible for anybody in the world to order a German language book, a Japanese language book—not just an English language book. So we need to have local customer service operations, local distribution centers, to really service those markets as if we were a local company there."[34]

Some companies have a unique skill set in providing professional advice. Ernst & Young started an online consulting program called Ernie. A subscriber can type questions into his computer and get a response to each one from an Ernst & Yong expert within forty-eight hours. For a subscription of $3,500 a year, five employees can ask a total of ten questions. For a subscription of $18,000, five employees can ask an unlimited number of questions.

Offering integrated solutions is another way that companies can win. Microsoft Office is a good example of this approach. It offers word processing, spreadsheets, and presentation capabilities in an integrated package. This is so important that a core design objective in many Microsoft products is seamless integration.[35]

Offering a "more for the same" value proposition is another effective approach. Lexus, for example, claims that the quality and performance of its products are comparable to those of Mercedes, BMW, and Jaguar, but its prices are much closer to those of the lower-end Cadillacs and Lincolns.

QUESTIONS TO PONDER

- Have you prepared a choice map of your customer's experience in obtaining your products and services? If not, outline how you would proceed.

- Develop a choice board that customers can use to order exactly what they want of your offerings. Would providing your customers this customization capability give your company a competitive advantage? What changes would your company have to make to implement the choice board?

- Can you think of a new form for delivering some customer benefit that was delivered in a traditional way?

- Have you made use of channel assembly or postponement to assemble offerings closer to each customer's preferences?

- What is your value proposition? Is it unique? Is it innovative?

FIVE

Designing the Business Architecture

The second set of basic building blocks—the company's competency space, the collaborators' resource space, the company's business domain, and the company's business partners—gives marketers strategic insight for designing the business architecture platform (see figure 5-1).

Two main engines drive the value stream in today's economy—the pull that comes from increasingly demanding consumers and the push that comes from innovative suppliers.

As discussed in chapter 4, consumers range from those who want to choose from a multitude of ready-to-buy products to those who seek to co-design or co-produce products to meet their specific needs. They range from those who make price-based purchasing decisions on commodities to those who make value-based purchasing decisions that provide individual solutions. At one extreme lies buyers and at the other lies co-producers. The spectrum runs from commodity buyer to product buyer, solution buyer, solution definer, solution co-designer, and finally, solution co-producer.

FIGURE 5-1   The Business Architecture Platform

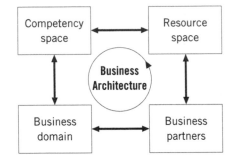

By the same token, suppliers vary from companies that operate throughout the entire value chain to specialists that focus on one particular domain of the chain. They vary from companies categorized by the outputs they produce (e.g., soap powder, automobiles) to those defined by the functions they perform in the chain (e.g., designers, packagers). At one extreme lie owners and at the other lie specialists. The spectrum runs from value network specialist to value network participant, value chain participant, value chain partner, value chain controller, and value chain owner.

In today's economy, many companies use digital technology and the Internet to streamline the processes, structure, and flow of products, services, and information among strategic partners. In this chapter, we discuss (1) generic business models, (2) B2C extended business models, and (3) B2B extended business models.

GENERIC BUSINESS MODELS

Companies design their business models in order to manage a particular value stream. Business can be conducted on a one-to-one, many-to-one, one-to-many, and many-to-many basis. Each type calls for a different architecture connecting the buyers and sellers.

One-to-One: Traditional E-Commerce without Intermediary

In the *one-to-one model*, the buyer and seller have a direct relationship. Today, this is enabled by digital technology helping companies to bypass middlemen in the value chain. For example, Amazon.com bypasses bookstores to sell one-to-one to each book buyer. The seller develops a simple channel extension and the buyers use Web-enabled purchasing. The company's revenue comes from cost-plus pricing and paid-for advertising.

Many-to-One: Buy-Side Intermediary

In the *many-to-one model*, the company acts as a buyer agent by aggregating many products of interest to buyers. Mohanbir Sawhney has called such sites *metamediaries*. Thus Edmunds.com assembles products and services of interest to auto buyers, and The Knot (theknot.com) assembles products and services of interest to those planning a wedding. Or the company might take on the role of a comparison aggregator by offering the ability to compare prices from many different producers for the same product, as does CompareNet. The company earns transaction fees and advertising fees.

Businesses have traditionally done their purchasing through professional buyers, who scanned catalogs, phoned suppliers, and worked to negotiate better terms. Modern purchasing agents are now adding cyber tools, creating their own buy-side intermediary to enhance their purchasing capabilities. General Electric, for example, created the Trading Process Network (TPN), through which GE, along with other subscribers to GE's service, can request quotes, negotiate terms, and place orders with global suppliers. Suppliers regularly visit this site to place bids for requested items. GE buyers claim that they are getting 10 to 15 percent cost savings through lower order-processing and purchasing costs.

Ford formed AutoXchange, a $300 million automotive e-business integrated supply chain, to reduce Ford's purchasing costs of $80 billion with its 30,000 suppliers while increasing its operating efficiency.[1]

One-to-Many: Sell-Side Intermediary

In the *one-to-many model,* the company acts on behalf of the seller or sellers. The company establishes relationships with preferred selling partners and receives a commission for its transactions. For example, Ingram Micro, the largest independent computer distributor in the world, uses Internet auctions to dispose of its seller clients' excess inventory.

Many-to-Many: Virtual Marketplace

Finally, in the *many-to-many model,* the company creates a wide forum connecting buyers and sellers. The company's revenue comes from advertising and transaction fees. For example, e-STEEL is a virtual marketplace for buying and selling steel products. eBay is an online exchange that allows buyers and sellers to transact over a diverse range of products. Users pay listing fees and a transaction percentage fee.

Many business designs are derived from the four generic models. From the middleman's perspective, there are three different processes. The first is *disintermediation,* in which existing middlemen are bypassed. Many physical stores that sell digital products such as music, software, travel, and theater tickets are in danger of being disintermediated. The second is *transintermediation,* in which established middlemen migrate to the Internet. Examples include brokerage businesses, employment agencies, dating services, and real estate agencies. The third is *reintermediation,* in which new types of middlemen set themselves up on the Internet. Examples include virtual sellers like CarPoint and Amazon.com, and Internet services such as Yahoo!, YesMail.com, Firefly, and iShip.[2]

B2C EXTENDED BUSINESS MODELS

There are several types of B2C business models. Here we highlight a few of them.

E-Commerce Storefronts

E-commerce storefronts are sites offering goods or services for sale. They succeed best when their offerings are suitable for e-tailing. Alex Birch, Philipp Herbert, Dirk Schneider, and their colleagues at the McKenna Group specify five highly suitable categories of offerings: (1) offerings that have lower transaction costs when they are traded online rather than in the physical world (e.g., books and software); (2) context-intensive offerings for which ancillary information is critical (e.g., travel and health products); (3) offerings that can use customer feedback to enhance and customize the product for the customer (e.g., computers and cars); (4) offerings with high built-in quality standards that do not need to be physically checked (e.g., many strong branded goods); and (5) offerings that have a high profit potential per unit (if they are being shipped).[3]

Portals and Infomediaries

Portals are gateways. Portals originally developed from temporary sites, such as search engines, and then grew into information centers providing news, opinions, and information. These changes were made to keep users on the sites longer so that they would view more pages, which in turn generated more advertising revenue.[4]

Infomediaries are a slight variation of the portal concept. In addition to providing specific information, an infomediary is usually a creator or a reseller of content. Infomediaries have a different model from e-tailers. Broadly, an infomediary is an entity that carries and brokers information, knowledge, or experiences. To the extent that Travelocity.com offers free travel information and Britannica.com offers free encyclopedia information, they are operating as infomediaries. Any supplier of content could be called an infomediary.

In *Net Worth*, John Hagel III and Marc Singer define infomediaries in a narrower sense, as sites that hold the consumer's private information and protect and manage it. When a Web site requests a set of data from the user, the user will refer the site to his or her infomediary site. The infomediary acts as a consumer custodian by evaluating the requested data each time. If the value of the data is high, the consumer custodian site might negotiate a special discount on behalf of the user in payment for the data. The infomediary's value lies both in privacy protection and in convenience; users don't have to retype their data every time they receive a request. The Web site owner also benefits, as the data it collects is of high quality.[5] (For examples of infomediaries, see www.job-search.engine.com, www.lumeria.com, and www.freeonline.com.)

America Online, Yahoo!, Lycos, and other portals are vying to be the first stop for access to the Internet. These portals are constantly transforming themselves into infomediaries, capturing information about users and, with this information, helping users connect with vendors.[6]

Facilitators

Facilitators are information providers that earn a modest transaction fee from matching buyers with sellers. A well-known example is eBay. Facilitators can package market offerings in different ways, say promising a special deal for some customers or offering selected customers more personalized and convenient service. Some companies view facilitators as additional channels for improving revenue, by expanding their coverage at a low cost and complementing their existing sales forces. Some telecommunications companies, for example, use facilitators to capture new customers. The facilitators draw on large databases of names, addresses, and telephone numbers to aggressively sell telecommunications products and services to a market that is usually untapped or ignored by conventional telecommunications selling practices.

Aggregators

Aggregators assemble information or supplies from several sources. Travelocity.com is an aggregator in that it posts the schedules of many airlines on their Web site. Edmunds.com is also an aggregator, listing information about every automobile currently on the market. Covisint is an aggregator in that it represents several auto companies and combines their intended purchase volumes of specific items to command deeper discounts from willing suppliers.

Both facilitators and aggregators create downward pressure on prices. They force traditional product-push companies to better leverage their customer information, improve customer service, and transform themselves into truly consumer-centric enterprises.[7]

Trust Intermediaries

Many consumers perceive online transactions as risky. "If goods are delivered, will they be the ones that were ordered? Can they be returned? To whom? At what cost?"[8]

In the case of purchasing books over the Internet, consumers perceive relatively little risk because of the low cost. Air travel, by contrast, not only costs hundreds of dollars but also is complicated by various factors such as routing, scheduling, and penalties for changes. The more important the purchase and the more unfavorable the consequence if things go wrong, the more the company needs to elicit trust.[9]

A *trust intermediary* is an entity that provides a secure environment in which buyers and sellers can confidently exchange value. There are two special types of trust infomediaries: payment enablers and trust enablers. *Payment enablers* ensure "payment transactions and reduce risks to buyers and sellers" while *trust enablers* "create a trusted or authenticated environment in which parties can interact with confidence and recourse."[10] Here is an example of a trust enabler:

ValueStar.com provides a seal of approval to a number of difficult-to-evaluate, un-standardized services such as auto repair, home contracting, and medical care. Visitors to the ValueStar site enter their zip codes and service needs. The service responds with approved vendors in the area. The ValueStar system is simple; no attempt is made to rank or rate the providers. The ValueStar seal is a stamp of approval, a positive recommendation.[11]

Digital technology allows for the creation of many competitive, anonymous markets. In an anonymous exchange, perfect information—not personal relationships—drives buying decisions and transactions in a lean, efficient manner. These markets cannot function without some level of trust. Two trust intermediaries are E-LOAN, which links mortgage brokers with lenders, and FastParts.com, which allows electronics manufacturers to exchange components.[12]

E-business Enablers

E-business enablers facilitate processes such as distribution and fulfillment in a partner's business operations. Examples include FedEx,

LoopNet, Egghead.com, and Chrome. When FedEx, for instance, provides the back-end, outbound fulfillment logistics for its clients, it is playing an e-business enabler role.

B2B EXTENDED BUSINESS MODELS

Here we discuss a few of the main B2B models.

B2B Portals

A *B2B portal* is a one-stop destination specific to an individual industry or function.

Industry portals include e-STEEL, e-Plastics, and others whose names often suggest their industries. *Function portals* include those that facilitate media buying, logistics, human resources services, and other business activities.

Business purchases can usually be grouped into manufacturing inputs and operating inputs. *Manufacturing inputs* include raw materials and components. Businesses may increasingly turn to digital marketplaces to purchase raw materials, such as steel or plastics. Components, on the other hand, may need to be designed and therefore purchased from specific manufacturers and distributors.

Operating inputs, often called maintenance, repair, and operating (MRO) items, include familiar products such as cleaning supplies, office supplies, and airline tickets. A broad range of businesses purchases these items. Companies selling these MRO items can set up online purchasing and use FedEx or UPS for delivery.[13]

A country can set up a portal to provide information about the products and services of its many manufacturers. China has set up MeetWorldTrade which features more than 15,000 electronic manufacturers in China who want to make their manufacturing services available to foreign firms. The site includes practical advice on cultural, financial, and human resources issues that a business anywhere in the world might want to consider.[14]

B2B Infomediary

A *B2B infomediary* is a Web site that creates, packages, and delivers information content to its own site and to others, including portals. Owned by Ziff Davis, ZDNet.com, which publishes computer and software information, is a good example of such an infomediary.[15]

B2B Hubs

A *hub* is a Web site set up to conduct e-commerce with a set of buyers and/or sellers. Steven Kaplan and Mohanbir Sawhney distinguish among four types of B2B hubs, as shown in figure 5-2.[16]

- A *yield manager hub* allows businesses to buy or sell operating inputs on a spot market basis, where prices and supplies vary daily. These hubs help suppliers who made high capital investments (such as public utilities selling electricity or airlines selling seats) to adjust their prices frequently to attract enough demand for their output capacity. YOUtilities.com is a good example of such a hub.

FIGURE 5-2   Kaplan and Sawhney's B2B Categories

	Spot Sourcing	Systematic Sourcing
Manufacturing Inputs	Exchange hubs	Catalog hubs
Operating Inputs	Yield manager hubs	Maintenance, repair, and operating hubs

Source: Adapted from Steven Kaplan and Mohanbir Sawhney, "E-Hubs: The New B2B Marketplaces," *Harvard Business Review* 78, no. 3 (May–June 2000): 99.

• An *MRO hub* (maintenance, repair, and operating supply industry) allows businesses to secure operating inputs of generally low value from specific suppliers. MRO hubs contribute to the business process by reducing transaction costs. Examples include W. W. Grainger and Ariba, both of which use third-party logistics firms to deliver the goods.

• An *exchange hub* allows buyers to connect and transact with sellers on a spot market basis to obtain specific manufacturing inputs. Examples include PaperSpace (for the paper industry) and Altra Energy (for the energy industry).

• A *catalog hub* allows buyers to view the catalogs and stated prices of industry-specific sellers. Catalog hubs contribute value by increasing customer convenience and reducing transaction costs. SciQuest (in the life-science industry) is a good example.

Table 5-1 lists five business models that B2B hubs currently use. These models will evolve according to the requirements of individual markets and operations.

Kaplan and Sawhney assert that e-hubs create value through the mechanisms of aggregation and matching.

TABLE 5-1   The Five B2B Models

Business Model	Transaction Type
Membership or subscription	Fixed annual fee or usage subscription base
Percentage of transaction	Share of transaction based on pre-agreed business model
Referral fee	Percentage based on agreed-fee basis
Auction	Based on auction rules for buyers and sellers of products in the exchange
Purchase of products/services	Based on transaction rules determined before entering and participating in the exchange

Source: Michael J. Cunningham, *B2B: How to Build a Profitable e-Commerce Strategy* (Cambridge, MA: Perseus Publishing, 2001), 18.

An *aggregation hub* brings together many buyers and sellers to deal in a fixed-price environment. The hub often features a mega-catalog of products carried by an array of suppliers. Aggregation works best when the products are specialized, when there is a high number of individual products, and when transaction costs are high relative to the cost of procuring the items.

A *matching hub* brings together many buyers and sellers to negotiate prices in real time. Participants list bids and asks on specific quantities of a product, and transactions take place when there is a match. Matching also occurs in auction hubs. Matching works best with products that are near commodities, where purchased volumes are large relative to transaction costs and demand and prices are normally volatile.

THE FUTURE OF B2B MARKETS

During the dot-com boom, observers expected companies to rush to do business on B2B hubs. Yet some B2B hubs have had to close their doors and others are struggling to survive. Richard Wise and David Morrison identified three factors that have inhibited the use of B2B hubs:[17]

1. Many companies have created partnerships with their best suppliers. Buying in these digital marketplaces, which often allows the companies to get lower prices, can undermine these well-established relationships.

2. Sellers whose prices are high relative to those of their competitors may hesitate to participate in these markets, where they would experience more price pressure. For these companies, the benefit of reaching more buyers cannot offset the greater price pressure.

3. Attracted by easy entry and low off-the-shelf software costs, many new competitors created e-hubs. The sudden influx hurt the margins of all competitors.

Yet Wise and Morrison forecast renewed growth of B2B hubs. They expect e-hubs to evolve toward handling more complex transactions and toward supporting solutions in addition to transactions. They see the emergence of e-speculators who will use real-time information to take advantage of price differences. And they expect the emergence of exchanges that will swap and resell orders among groups of member buyers.

From the very beginning of online transactions, forecasters such as Forrester Research and Gartner predicted that B2B businesses would grow ten to fifteen times larger than B2C businesses. This will play out as more company purchasing departments recognize the cost savings inherent in doing a larger proportion of their purchases online and as they gain the skills to manage procurement in a digital-intense economy.

QUESTIONS TO PONDER:

- Should your business add e-commerce capacity and sell online? What value will your company create for its customers and suppliers by offering e-commerce? If your business is currently selling through agents and retailers, how can it retain their allegiance if it decides to sell online?

- How can your company use the power of e-procurement to lower its input purchase costs? On what types of e-hubs would you focus?

Building the Business Infrastructure and Capabilities

In the "we make it, you take it" model of business, products and communications moved mostly one way, from producers to customers, through limited channels. Senior management dictated what, when, and how to sell. Today, with the emergence of the Internet, communications have become two way, that is, *interactive*. Customers can know more about companies, and companies can accumulate fuller information about their customers. The richer information enables companies to establish stronger relationships with their customers and collaborators. Such relationships can be harnessed to explore new business opportunities, as well as to build stronger competitive advantage. In order to manage customer and collaborator relationships more efficiently and effectively, companies need to renew their business infrastructures and capabilities by investing in three systems: (1) customer relationship management (CRM), (2) internal resource management (IRM), and (3) business partnership management (BPM).

CUSTOMER RELATIONSHIP MANAGEMENT

All companies would like to develop a solid base of "good" customers who would:

- buy more from the company, even if its prices are relatively higher than competitors' prices;

- become apostles, recommending the company and its products to colleagues, family, and friends;

- make the company the standard for the organization or family;

- try out the company's new offerings and help the company make them better; and

- use company support, service, and other facilities.

To reach and retain such customers, many companies are moving from product management to customer management and are focusing on managing interactions with individual customers. In the industrial age, companies bore high costs in maintaining close relationships with their individual customers. These costs hindered the creation of relationship and personalized services. Today, companies can build and maintain individual customer relationships at a much lower cost.

Arthur M. Hughes has identified five criteria for successful CRM: (1) the company has well-developed marketing processes; (2) the company can easily capture customers' names, addresses, and purchase behavior; (3) data about customers' repeat-purchases can be captured at the point of sale; (4) the company has the skills to build and mine their databases; and (5) the company can offer a frequency reward program with significant benefits for both parties.[1]

A great number of businesses meet these criteria, including automobile companies, hotels, airlines, financial companies, and retail establishments. But Hughes noted two types of products that are

TABLE 6-1   The Customer Relationship Management Process

Stage of Customer Relationship Management	Key Initiatives
Finding the target customers	• Defining target markets • Acquiring target customers
Filling the target customers' needs	• Translating the customer value into actionable customer benefits • Matching the market offerings with the customer's choice context
Forming the link with target customers	• Designing market intelligence • Gaining insights from customer information

unlikely candidates for CRM: commodity products (such as soft drinks or spices) with too slim a margin to finance relationship-building activity, and products that are purchased infrequently (grand pianos or major works of art) and at unpredictable times.

Carrying out a CRM program is a three-stage process: (1) finding the target customers, (2) filling the target customers' needs, and (3) forming long-lasting links with the target customers (see table 6-1).

Finding the Target Customers

Finding the target customers involves defining the target market and acquiring target customers.

Defining the target market. All marketing, including CRM, starts with defining the target market. Over time, as competitive intensity has increased, market segments have become smaller and more fragmented. Fortunately, digital technology allows companies to micro-segment their customers. Consider the following examples:[2]

• Dell microsegments its customers by setting up different access sites from different countries. Further, it provides customized "stores" for each customer type: home; small business; business; health care; higher education; K–12 education; and federal, state, and local government. Dell can track customers by the products they buy: notebooks, desktops, servers and storage, workstations, software, and add-ons. The company's online auction site, Dell Factory Outlet, provides additional layers of customer segmentation by attracting customers who want to buy and sell preowned and refurbished Dell systems. Dell provides customized interfaces as well as additional services to those of its customers who are registered as members, and it offers Premier Dell.com for its corporate and institutional customers.

• The magazine *Sports Illustrated* classifies its readers into four "customer experience" groups: those who want pure escape, those looking for a source of sports trivia, those seeking collectibles, or those who want a how-to guide. It then extends those experiences with specialized lines of books, videos, CD-ROMs, a kids' magazine, and travel packages to sporting events.

Acquiring target customers. Companies need to identify the right target customers within each target market. In order to do so, marketers must periodically review their assumptions about who the buyer is. For years, Kodak had sold X-ray film to hospital lab technicians, but it was late in noticing that the purchase decision was increasingly shifting to professional administrators. And Reuters had focused on selling its news services and standardized systems to IT managers, but Bloomberg came along and created systems for traders and analysts that went far beyond the standardized systems that the IT managers had been purchasing.[3]

After identifying target customers, companies must answer two questions about them: Do the target customers want a close relationship with the company? and Does the company want a close relationship with all the customers?

Not all customers are equally valuable. Marketers need to grade their customers by profitability, as measured by lifetime value, and allocate more attention to the more valuable customers. Figure 6-1 shows two ways of analyzing a customer's profitability, one by the current situation and the other by the future situation.

There are additional ways of measuring a customer's profitability. Here is one company's classification of prospects and customers by their value to the firm in terms of sales revenue:[4]

- *Platinum* ("top" customers): the top 1 percent of the company's active customers

- *Gold* ("big" customers): the next 4 percent of active customers

- *Iron* ("medium" customers): the next 15 percent of active customers

---

FIGURE 6-1   Analyzing Customer Profitability

A. Current Situation

	High Current Profitability	Low Current Profitability
Low Cost to Serve	Most profitable customers	Profitable customers
High Cost to Serve	Profitable customers	Least profitable customers

B. Future Situation

	High Current Profitability	Low Current Profitability
High Future Profitability	Best customers	Invest customers
Low Future Profitability	Maintain customers	Worst customers

- *Lead* ("small" customers): the remaining 80 percent of active customers

Marketers should spend more to reach and serve the higher-value prospects. A company might spend $3 contacting each high-value prospect, of which there are 20 ($60), and $1 contacting each low-value prospect, of which there are 500 ($500). Such targeted marketing will produce better results than spending the same amount of money to mail a generic brochure to all prospects.

Here are some interesting findings analyzed by Jay and Adam Curry:[5]

- The top 20 percent of customers deliver 80 percent of revenues but may deliver more than 100 percent of profits.

- Existing customers deliver up to 90 percent of revenues.

- A large portion of marketing budgets is often spent on noncustomers.

- Between 5 and 30 percent of all customers have the potential for upgrading in the customer pyramid.

- Customer satisfaction is critical for migration up the pyramid.

- A 2 percent upward migration in the customer pyramid can mean 10 percent more revenues and 50 percent more profit.

Ultimately, the value of a customer is revealed not by a single purchase but by the customer's expected purchases over the customer lifetime. *Customer lifetime value* (CLV) describes the present value of the stream of future profits expected over the customer's purchase lifetime. The company must subtract from the expected period revenues the expected period costs of attracting, selling, and servicing that customer.

Various CLV estimates have been made for different products and services. In *Customers for Life*, Carl Sewell estimated that a customer entering his car dealership for the first time represents a potential lifetime value of over $300,000.[6] This number represents the CLV if the customer is satisfied and buys several automobiles from the dealership over his or her buying lifetime. If the customer brings in other customers, the figure could be even higher. Mark Grainer, former chairman of the Technical Assistance Research Programs Institute, estimated that a loyal supermarket customer is worth $3,800 annually.[7]

In addition to an average customer estimate, of course, a company needs a way of estimating CLV for each individual customer in order to decide how much to invest in each one.

Filling the Target Customers' Needs

Having found its target customers, the company's next task is to fill their needs. This involves translating customer value into actionable customer benefits and matching the market offerings and communications with the individual customer's choice context.

Translating customer value into actionable customer benefits. Businesses today are increasingly focused on finding out what customers want. Marketers must be able to translate customer wants into individual actionable customer benefits. From the customer's perspective, the benefit from a purchase can be described as follows:[8]

Customer benefit = u (utility of market offering) + b (value of brand) + r (value of relationship) − c (cost of market offering) − t (cost of time)

The coefficients u, b, r, c, and t can be viewed as weights that vary across customer segments. Business-to-business buyers may place the highest weight on u, c, and t. Low-income customers may place a higher weight on c and a lower weight on u and t. Buyers also will place varying weights on r. Marketers, therefore, can position an offering based on the estimated coefficients for the target customer. The company needs to define target markets made up of customers driven by similar weights so that it can design appropriate offerings.

Matching the market offerings with the customer's choice context. Positioning the market offering must also take into account the customer's *choice context*. For example, buyers of notebook computers may also be interested in related products and services, such as printers and extended warranties. Or when consumers order basic long-distance telephone service, they may also consider adding Internet access. The cross-selling opportunity is determined by the customer's needs-based segment, usage pattern, and response to previous contacts.

To understand their customers' experiential context, marketers should develop choice maps. We distinguish three types of offerings:

1. Offerings that stand alone and provide positive net present value and relationship value.

2. Offerings that contribute no net present value by themselves but that help to develop and strengthen some of the value-contributing relationships. These offerings act like loss leaders. Many accounting firms, for example, offer free consulting services to attract new audit clients. Any client that takes advantage of the service is likely to remain with the accounting firm for years, thus repaying the initial investment.

3. Offerings that typically represent a one-time transaction and create no relationship value. Examples might include big-ticket durable goods, real estate brokerage, corporate financing deals, and commodities trading.

The roles of these various offerings may change over time. A new client attracted by the free consulting offer may not stay with the firm very long, so the firm will not realize eventual profit from the free-service loss leader. Today, instead of focusing on the product life cycle, marketers can focus on the targeted customer life cycle. Different stages in the customer's life cycle involve different contextual experience and thus demand different market offerings.

To develop longer lasting customers, a company should apply value-based segmentation, need-based segmentation, and predictive churn models, in that order. *Value-based segmentation* enables the company to determine the optimal amount it should invest to retain each customer. Knowing that, the company then applies *need-based segmentation* to develop appropriate offerings. Finally, the company uses *predictive churn models* to predict customer vulnerability. Vulnerable customers that are worth saving can be offered certain "free" services or lower prices.

Forming the Link with Target Customers

The final task in matching the market offerings with the customer's choice context is to build a more satisfying and lasting relationship with valued customers. This calls for investments in improving the company's market intelligence.

Designing market intelligence. CRM cannot work without market intelligence systems that capture data about customers' buying patterns, demographics, psychographics, and company contacts. Knowledge is information that has been edited, put into context, and analyzed in a way that makes it meaningful. Successful companies create collaborative networks to gain and disseminate this knowledge. Consider the following examples:[9]

- Dell Computer learns about customer preferences by studying which products and features customers select. This information enhances Dell's ability to price and promote different configurations aggressively.

- Amazon.com not only studies what individual users browse and buy, but it also integrates this data from users with similar patterns to make new recommendations to individual customers.

- General Motors consolidated customer databases from its various divisions into a single database and is using that information to create new car models with overlapping target markets across brands. This database consolidation, along with a reduction in the number of customer call centers from sixty to three, helps GM provide reliable, centralized customer service.

Marketers should reduce the time between acquiring information and translating that information into market offerings. For example, many ATMs feature messages such as "Call our toll-free number for information about such and such." But when clients call the number, the customer service rep who answers usually has no information about the customer's history or the particular sales promotion. It would be better for an ATM to inform a customer, "We see that you have $5,000 over the required balance in your account. Would you like us to move that money into a higher-interest-bearing money market account?" or "Interest rates have dropped 1 percent. Would you like to speak with a bank representative about refinancing your mortgage to save $2,000 annually in interest costs?" Such flawless transfer of customer information enhances the lifetime value of the customer both by increasing customer satisfaction and by increasing the sales of products and services.[10]

Gaining insights from customer information. Today, more companies view their individual customer information as a strategic asset for sustaining their competitive advantage. They adopt data-warehousing and data-mining techniques to deepen their understanding of an individual customer's behavior, emerging needs, and consumption patterns.

Each company must define the customer information it needs to *warehouse,* or accumulate. The most important information to track is the customers' purchases and inquiries, which indicate their needs and preferences. If possible, the company should also capture demographic data on age, education, and income. Often this information can be purchased from credit firms. Psychological data on the buyer's activities (such as golf or tennis), interests (such as listening to music or reading novels), and opinions (conservative or liberal) can be helpful, especially in business-to-customer settings. The market intelligence systems must be set up to capture this data from multiple sources such as transactions (preferences and purchase frequency), customer behavior (click-and-search patterns), and direct inquiries (profile data or surveys). The data is integrated, warehoused, and shared across market-facing activities such as marketing, sales, and customer service.

Data mining uses high-powered analytical and statistical techniques, such as neutral networking, automatic interaction detection, and cluster analysis, to reveal meaningful patterns and findings about customers. *Click-stream data,* for instance, shows each individual (unknown) user's patterns of clicking through the company's Web site. *Collaborative filtering applications* compile target customers' preferences and make recommendations based on correlating user taste preferences. CDNOW.com can recommend specific music to a customer based on what similar customers have purchased. *Rules-based systems* use customer profile data to identify appropriate messages or content to send to profiled users.[11]

To mine data successfully requires having sound statistical techniques and using them skillfully. Different data-mining analysts can come up with quite different findings. What companies need is not technicians who want only to drive a database (output) but analysts who want to drive the business (outcome). Here are some successful examples:[12]

- Bank of America managers can access individual customer profiles to cross-sell products while customers are still in the bank.

- The bank MBNA has increased its profits sixteenfold by reducing its customer attrition rate to half the industry average and by focusing on its more profitable customers.

- 1-800-FLOWERS.com maximizes its customer profitability and usage by automatically reminding individual customers of their important personal dates (e.g., birthdays, anniversaries).

- Hertz continually monitors competitive information (through intelligent agent technology) to react quickly to changing market conditions.

- Lands' End mails different catalogs to its various customer segments and carefully monitors customer purchase response performance in order to improve future product offerings.

Market intelligence can be used to suggest a needed promotional campaign, to alert marketers to make a timely phone call to a customer, or to evaluate the effectiveness of a pricing program. To reap these kinds of benefits, however, the company's staff must believe in and act on the value of collecting and analyzing this information.

Building and using a customer database will require substantial changes in management practices. Departmental data must flow into a centralized information system. The information must be easily accessible to different levels of management with appropriate passwords. Managers must begin to see themselves as knowledge workers operating in a learning culture.

INTERNAL RESOURCE MANAGEMENT

Going beyond CRM, a company also needs to improve management of its internal resources. The goal of IRM is to reduce working capital, shorten cycle times, and improve overall operations by better managing the company's human, financial, and physical capital. Instead of many fragmented software pieces disconnected from one another, managers need a common platform to integrate a broad range of disparate technologies. Such platforms are called *enterprise resource planning* (ERP) and *supply chain management* (SCM) systems. Using IRM software, the company can record the financial impact of a sale, the insourcing of the physical inputs, and the flow of the physical outputs through appropriate warehouses and transportation.

The Swedish communications company Ericsson sees IRM as a major step in its migration from a functional-based organization to a truly integrated one. Ericsson aims to make accessible a single integrated view of all its information: general ledger, accounts payable and receivable, order entry, billing systems, sales, marketing, materials, purchasing, product data management, shop floor control, and manufacturing operations.[13] The company has reported the following significant performance improvements:[14]

- On-time delivery of 98 percent of orders

- Reduction of sales order-processing lead time from one hour to ten minutes

- Reduction of purchase order lead time from one to four hours to less than five minutes

As a key driver of the value chain, IRM is supported by e-business technologies. Companies can purchase IRM software, from vendors such as Oracle, SAP, and PeopleSoft, that provides a wide range of functions for running a company's applications and delivering value to its customers.[15] IRM vendors use e-business technologies to interconnect companies with their business partners, both upstream to suppliers' information systems and downstream into distributors' and customers' information systems.[16] This allows, for instance, companies to provide customers with information on the status of their orders in the manufacturing process and on expected delivery time.

BUSINESS PARTNERSHIP MANAGEMENT

Successful companies today work with a large set of business partners that make up the company's collaborative network. The network, according to the authors of *Executive's Guide to E-Business,* comprises the following six types of partners:[17]

1. *Strategic service partners* provide outsourced business processes for their customers. Many supermarkets, for instance, contract with strategic service partner specialists to develop private-label versions of national brands. Pharmaceutical companies may contract with them for outside research and development on certain projects.

2. *Nonstrategic service partners* provide commodity-type administrative and other non-core business functions, including accounting, finance, human resources, indirect procurement, and travel.

3. *Value-added suppliers* provide engineered or configured parts or subassemblies specific to a client's requirements. A company's value-added suppliers usually provide early consultation on design and development requirements.

4. *Commodity suppliers* provide basic components and subassemblies. Many commodity suppliers perceive the Internet as a threat because buyers can click to find the lowest cost commodity suppliers.

5. *Network operations* partners provide a secure, high-speed backbone to connect the companies in the collaborative network. They enhance the companies' capabilities by providing links, standards, and interfaces that integrate the partners. They provide the required computing and network hardware, arrange secure network connectivity to authorized users, take responsibility for ongoing IT operations, assist in scaling and upgrading the system, and provide integration templates to connect network partners.

6. *Application service providers* provide and manage packaged application software to customers from central data facilities.

A company needs to develop trusted business partners who will share in making significant investments and commitments. Cisco Systems provides a good example.

Cisco works with its business partners through an Internet-based management system. Through *co-specialization* they create value by pooling the previously separate resources, skills, and knowledge. Cisco can then focus on a narrow range of core skills and activities, leaving manufacturing and other functions to its partners. The network is based on such partnership practices as information sharing, high levels of collaboration, and mutual trust.[18]

Companies in business partnerships must recognize that harmony may not be the most important goal. Occasional conflict may be the best evidence of mutually beneficial collaboration as well as a source of new ideas.

As their relationships grow closer, partners grow more interdependent on information flows. This interdependency leads to a major shift in the competitive landscape, from manufacturer-based competition to collaborative network-based competition. This shift, in turn, forces other companies to solidify relationships with their own partners in order to sustain their competitiveness.

Leading companies are often the most innovative in their collaborative networks. Here are two examples:

- Dell Computer has pursued a customer-responsive order-fulfillment strategy. Dell depends on its suppliers to make the components and get them to Dell on time. "We already have a quick-ship plan for large customers, where we can deliver a machine within 48 hours of an order," says Michael Dell.[19] The free flow of information through the collaborative network is the heart of Dell's strategy.

- Procter & Gamble (P&G) plays its supply chain like a maestro. The company works with its suppliers and distributors to create business plans and operations that reduce wasteful practices across the entire supply chain. P&G estimates that it saves retail customers millions of dollars annually through efficiency gains throughout the chain.

Martin Deise, Conrad Nowikow, Patrick King, and Amy Wright distinguish three forms of collaborative network relationships: commodity-based relationships, strategic relationships, and market-facing relationships.[20]

Commodity-based relationships are a company's relationships with suppliers that provide commodity products used either as operating inputs or as basic manufacturing inputs. The company selects vendors on the basis of cost and service, also taking into account availability and transport distance. The Internet is playing a growing role in scheduling and purchasing commodity materials. The speedier and richer information and communication it provides allows companies to manage with less on-hand inventory. Vendors increasingly take responsibility for managing their customers' inventories in a system known as *vendor-managed inventory* (VMI). The company shares its demand forecasts, current inventory levels, and logistics information with its major suppliers. This information allows the suppliers to determine when to refill inventory levels and send shipment notices.

As a result, VMI promises to reduce cycle time, head counts, and costs while at the same time improving accuracy.[21]

Strategic relationships are partnerships with companies that supply noncommodity inputs to the production and delivery process. Intel is a strategic partner of IBM in supplying proprietary chips. FedEx is a strategic partner of the online florist Calyx & Corolla in that the latter's business depends on FedEx's performance. ACNielsen is a strategic partner of Kraft Foods in that it provides early marketing data that enables Kraft to respond swiftly to market trends.[22]

The Internet plays a major role in linking the company to its strategic suppliers through programs such as VMI and collaborative planning, forecasting, and replenishment (CPFR). During product development, suppliers and companies use the Internet to perform the concurrent engineering required to orchestrate collaborative planning. The Internet is also used to communicate long-term pricing agreements and blanket purchase orders between companies and suppliers.

Market-facing relationships are partnerships in which companies work jointly or as part of a consortium to deliver a bundle of products and services. Thus, a group of hospital suppliers may develop a Web site allowing hospital purchase agents to procure medical supplies from them.

CROSS-FUNCTIONAL INTEGRATION APPLICATIONS

E-business is leading to a total overhaul of enterprise and intercompany systems. Companies are now installing *application clusters*, which integrate an array of internal functions including enterprise resource planning (e.g., SAP), customer relationship management (e.g., Siebel Systems), supply chain management (e.g., i2 Technologies), selling chain management (e.g., Trilogy), and operating resource management (e.g., Ariba).

Companies do not need a software vendor so much as a partner to handle these business applications. As Pete Hitchen, senior Internet analyst at IDC, has pointed out, "You need a partner who'll keep pace with the trends. You just can't buy brand-name software. You have to buy from someone who knows your industry."

Each supplier of application software positions itself as having distinct competencies and value to its customers. Oracle, for example, boasts that it transforms its clients' administrative process into self-service kiosks, connects internal information to external stakeholders, and turns transactions into business intelligence. It provides CRM to centrally track all interactions between a company and its clients. Oracle's key markets are automotive, aviation, defense, communications, petroleum, financial, health, pharmaceuticals, public service, and utilities.

Ariba, on the other hand, links buyers and sellers online through its Operating Resource Management System. Ariba's key markets are consumer, petroleum, telecommunications, public service, high technology, financial, and transport.[23]

Technology has enabled management to make better decisions in such areas as demand planning, transportation planning, distribution planning, order commitment, and advanced scheduling. But companies need more than just software. They need skills in business partner management if they are to achieve peak performance.[24]

QUESTIONS TO PONDER

- How practical is it for your business to adopt the CRM perspective and deal with your customers on a one-to-one basis?

- Does your company have a satisfactory system for estimating customer lifetime value? What are the obstacles?

- Does your company classify customers into profitability levels? What method do you use? Can you improve it?

- How can your company use the Internet to get better leads and to achieve a deeper understanding of customers' needs?

- Has your company set up an intranet? What are its main uses and benefits? What are its main limitations?

- Has your company moved into IRM (such as ERP, SCM, or CRM)? If not, why? What would you invest in first, and what results would you expect?

- With which distributors and suppliers should your company build electronic information and transaction links?

- Has your company developed sufficiently strong links among its own departments to ensure that the company's business partnership management system is effective?

SEVEN

Designing the Marketing Activities

In the industrial age, marketers relied on the framework of the Four Ps—product, price, place, and promotion—to develop a marketing plan for their customers. Companies created the products and defined their features and benefits; set prices; selected places to sell products and services; and promoted intrusively through advertising, public relations, and direct mail. The underlying paradigm was one of unidirectional control.

What will the Four P marketing mix mean in the digital economy? Digital technology and multimedia, because they provide comprehensive information and allow one-to-one interactions, enrich the opportunities for all marketing activities. The standard multimedia browser, the software that interfaces to the Internet, may become the "killer application" in achieving new levels of marketing performance.[1]

Furthermore, as the ubiquity of the Internet becomes a reality, a new kind of intermediary role emerges: the *mobilemediary*. These mobilemediaries (e.g., mobile phones, personal digital assistants,

FIGURE 7-1   The Marketing Activities Platform

pagers, etc.) use many digital tools (e.g., electronic wallets, smart cards, mobile shopping lists, and Internet-enabled point-of-sale systems) to extend marketing's reach beyond the desktop computer and to enrich customers' experiences in both the physical and the virtual worlds.

The next set of basic building blocks—the customer benefits, the company's business domain, customer relationship management, and internal resource management—gives marketers insight for designing marketing activities (see figure 7-1). In this chapter, we discuss the shifts in managing major marketing activities in the digital economy, covering channels, promotion, and pricing. We have discussed the issues in designing product offerings in previous chapters.

MANAGING CHANNELS

The number of distribution channels has mushroomed, and companies must be prepared to manage more channels, in addition to modifying their offerings and pricing in the different channels. Here we consider some of the major channel issues and opportunities.

Resolving Channel Conflict

The Internet represents a new channel for information, two-way communications, and sales. Pure-click companies have no problem selling online, but established companies with dealer networks encounter strong objections to adding online sales. Established companies struggle with the question of how to conduct online sales without cannibalizing their stores, resellers, or agents. Here are ways that some companies have resolved this conflict:

- When Talbots, a specialty women's clothing chain, is out of a store item, a salesclerk can order it from the store's catalog call center. Since the $4 flat shipping charge for call-center orders is less than the $5 to $14 for regular catalog orders, customers are motivated to place the order and the store earns credit for the catalog sale.[2]

- Liberty Mutual finds out from each online customer whether he or she prefers to buy directly or through a financial adviser. If the latter, the customer's information is routed to an adviser.[3]

- Avon could not ignore the vast potential of the Internet. Fortunately, the company's research showed little overlap between existing customers and potential Internet customers, so Avon established a Web site. Meanwhile, the company also offered to help its reps set up their own Web sites so they could augment their sales as well.[4]

- Gibson Guitars could not sell guitars online due to conflict with its dealers, but it could sell accessories such as guitar strings and parts directly to consumers.[5]

- J. C. Penney uses its Web site to offer online coupons that can be printed and redeemed at its stores. Penney also might add offerings online that would not be profitable to sell through its stores.[6]

Developing an Attractive and Effective Company Web Site

A company's Web site will serve as an effective channel for providing information, conducting transactions, and building relationships with its customers, business partners, and various other segments of the public. It should reflect the best of the company's quality, service, and speed. For example, Disney has been using its Web site to promote the Disney brand franchise, the brand image of each Disney character, and its children's programming on its ABC television network. And Procter & Gamble has actively developed attractively designed individual Web sites for such brands as Crest, NyQuil, Vicks, Sunny Delight, Folgers, and Charmin.[7]

A great many current Web sites, however, are not user friendly. Many do not focus on meeting users' or visitors' needs. In "Why Most Websites Fail," Forrester reports that of every one million unique visitors per month, 40 percent are driven away by hard-to-read text, slow performance, or poor reliability. The report also shows that a user who has had a bad experience with a Web site typically tells several other people.[8]

Companies should invite customer feedback in order to improve its site. Yahoo!, for example, invited users on several occasions to comment on new services. Amazon invited its customers to help test a new navigation system. Some Internet sites, such as Amazon.com and CDNOW.com, welcome customer reviews of books, music, and other items that are then shared with all the other visitors to the site. Listening to customers provides critical input for developing successful businesses.[9]

The existence of interactive communities allows companies to learn from customer criticism. Here is a case in which Intel ignored customer criticism, to its dismay:

In the mid '90s a group of scientists showed that one of Intel's new generation of microprocessors could miscalculate when dealing with very large numbers and told the company about the mistake. The company ignored their advice. The phenomenon was rapidly discussed by the scientists over the Internet and the defect was confirmed by many more experts. In a concerted action they sent hundreds of e-mails to Intel, who replied back with standard e-mail. The story was then leaked to the press, and reported in news broadcasts all over the world, creating real damage to Intel's image.[10]

Companies should strive to develop Web sites that create "flow experiences" for their users. The greater the flow experience, the higher the possibility of raising customer service and satisfaction to new levels. Reliable exchanges of information continuously flowing between the company and its customers will encourage customers to view the company as a valuable resource and will increase their loyalty.

It is comparatively easy to attract a visitor to the company's Web site once: Just spend a lot of money on offline and online advertising or offer something free online. Most dot-coms pursued this goal, and some succeeded admirably. Amazon, for example, claims that 23 million visitors have visited its site one or more times.

But visits are one goal; repeat visitors are another. Companies must create Web sites that visitors want to visit again and again. Venture capital firms and other investors judge the quality of a site's audience by that site's depth-of-repeat characteristics. This information comes from the site's browser, which deposits a cookie on a visitor's computer that then records his or her every visit.

Making a company's Web site compelling requires managing both context and content factors.

Context factors. Visitors will judge a site's performance on its ease of use and its physical attractiveness. Its *ease of use* hinges on the following attributes:

• The site downloads quickly.

• The first page is easy to understand.

• The site is easy to navigate, and its pages open quickly.

The site's *physical attractiveness* is determined by the following factors:

• The individual pages are clean and not overly crammed with content.

• The typefaces and font sizes are readable online.

• The site makes good use of color and sound.

Content factors. The preceding context factors facilitate but do not ensure repeat visits to a Web site. Content is what encourages return visits—it must be interesting, useful, and continuously changing. Certain types of content function well to attract first-time visitors and to bring them back again:

• Deep information with links to related sites

• Changing news of interest

• Changing free offers

• Contests and sweepstakes

• Humor and jokes

• Games

From time to time, the company should reevaluate its site's attractiveness and usefulness. One way to do this is by inviting the opinions of Web site design experts. But the more important source of information is users, who can be asked what they like and dislike about the site and invited to make suggestions for improving it.

Engaging in Customer-Interactive Communities

Companies can take advantage of customer-interactive communities to enter into dialogue with their customers. They can build network hubs to create good word of mouth about their market offerings. Apple, for example, feels like a club to its "members," and Saturn is a club of car owners.[11] When individuals become familiar with and interact with the company, a community grows.

The many kinds of communities include demographic communities (e.g., tripod.com, which targets people of ages twenty-five to thirty), geographical communities (e.g., mauritius.net), industry-specific communities (e.g., textilefind.com for the textile industry), function-oriented communities (e.g., monster.com helps in job searching and recruiting), and subject-oriented communities (e.g., espn.com, a very large sports-oriented site).[12]

Community is a dynamic concept. Many communities divide to form subcommunities by segmenting an extensive subject into specific topics, sometimes with different Internet addresses. The number of subcommunities associated with a site is termed the *fractal depth* of a community. Alternatively, one type of community may give rise to another type, called its *fractal breadth*. For example, a geographical community may give rise to a subject-oriented subcommunity, or a demographic community may extend into a geographic one. The charm and market potential of a site varies proportionately with these factors.[13]

Companies can benefit from building *virtual communities* of customers who interact not just with them but also with one another. Communities have a number of specific advantages over commercial Web sites. Online communities accumulate information about individual members' interests, activities, and needs over time. This information, along with interaction with members, can improve a company's ability to tailor its offerings to the specific needs of its members. Consumers with similar interests gather at such communities, making it more convenient for companies to tailor their messages to current and potential customers. By allowing customers to access relevant product information and discuss it online with experienced users, communities reduce uncertainty about the product and increase customers' willingness to buy. Companies can also eliminate the need for middlemen by communicating interactively and building relationships with end users. Most airlines have established direct booking systems for customers via the Internet, bypassing the traditional travel agents.[14]

It is easy to establish simple discussion communities for users of purchased goods (e.g., software packages). Members of these communities may provide helpful advice to one another, and companies can identify issues and improve offerings through the members' problems and complaints.

Community sponsors should take the next step, actively participating in and identifying with the goals of the community. Cisco Systems, for example, enables customers to provide input for Cisco products and to help other customers, which has helped Cisco reduce its maintenance and customer-support costs.[15] Cisco has transformed its community of users into a community of value. The next step is to transform a community of value into *communities of requirements,* in which individual's needs can be satisfied.[16]

Building an online community, however, requires considerable resources, often more than many companies have. Yet delaying the move may be dangerous. As Candice Carpenter, CEO of iVillage, warned, "If a company has not created an on-line community brand within the next 12 months, then it has no chance of doing so."[17]

Creating Word of Mouth through Network Hubs

Network hubs are individuals who communicate with more people about a certain market offering than the average person does. Other terms for network hubs are *opinion leaders, influencers, lead users,* and *power users.* Network hubs may or may not be the first to adopt new products, but they have a great influence on future purchases.

Everett Rogers points out that network hubs are more "cosmopolite" than others. They tend to be connected with others outside the local system. Network hubs in the high-tech industry, for example, are connected to other network hubs from whom they can get more information. Such people can be found by visiting relevant trade shows and joining user groups and online forums; network hubs in turn lead to additional links to the outside world.[18]

Word of mouth, or *buzz,* is critical in many businesses. To stimulate word of mouth, marketers should identify the network hubs from whom customers typically learn about the company's market offerings. In addition, companies need to know:[19]

- What do people say when they recommend the company's product?

- How fast does information about the company's product spread compared with other products?

- When does the information hit a roadblock?

- How many sources of information does a customer rely on? Which ones are more important?

- What other kinds of information spread through the same networks?

The importance of word of mouth varies from business to business. Products that lend themselves to high customer involvement can be exciting products like books, records, and movies; innovative products like the Walkman and the Palm organizer; personal-experience products like hotels, airlines, and cars; complex products like software and medical devices; expensive products like computers and consumer electronics; and observable products like apparel, cars, and cellular phones.[20]

MANAGING PROMOTION

Promotion has traditionally involved heavy expenditures on advertising and sales promotion in B2C markets and heavy expenditures on personal selling in B2B markets. Today, companies are reexamining these practices. In the case of mass advertising, much of which is television based, companies are coming to recognize that the proliferation of channels, the practice of zapping, and the decreased time people spend watching TV are diminishing their exposure. Consumers are paying increasing attention to radio ads (as traffic congestion keeps people in their cars longer) and to magazines, which are better able to reach targeted audiences.

Businesses selling to other businesses recognize that their sales forces are their largest marketing expense so are taking steps to moderate the costs associated with them. Salespeople are being retrained from being skilled at persuasion to being skilled at listening, proposing solutions, and adding value to their customers' businesses. Companies are replacing some field salespeople with telemarketers, especially for prospecting, reaching, and servicing smaller customers. Companies hope that their Web sites will provide considerable information so that their sales forces will be able to spend less time describing the company and its offerings and more time consulting with customers on how to improve their profitability. Dell salespeople, for example, show clients and prospects how they can lower their computerization costs by buying Dell PCs.

Digital technology can reduce the need for customer service representatives to answer customers' questions. Cisco and other companies have developed lists of Frequently Asked Questions (FAQs) that they can download to inquiring customers. FAQs can cover a wide range of topics, from the overtly technical to the covertly encouraging. FAQs are also an objective and neutral means of imparting critical information about issues such as payment conditions and data protection. A good FAQ list, such as the one the U.S. Postal Service's

Web site, offers links to additional information in response to relevant questions.[21]

Companies are also recognizing the power of direct marketing to communicate much of their message through the phone, the mail, and the Internet. They are using public relations tools—newsletters, press releases, events, and sponsorships—to capture attention and create buzz in the marketplace and marketspace. And they are using their databases, data mining, automatic computer dialing, and e-mail to build a brand relationship with their target customers.

In the past, communication budgets and tools were poorly integrated. Today, there is a much welcome movement toward integrated marketing communications. Companies need to harness all of their communication channels to deliver a consistent value proposition to their target market.

Online advertising has grown rapidly and has taken on many forms. Here are some of them.

Banner ads. The most extensively used advertising platform on the Internet is *banner ads*. These ads appear as small boxes containing a little text and perhaps a picture. Most are fairly static, although some are animated to attract attention. Companies pay Web sites fees to place their banner ads on those sites. The larger the Web site's audience, the higher the cost of the banner placement. Popular portals such as Yahoo! and America Online can charge large fees to companies placing banners on their sites. But the fees may be coming down. As recently as 1999, as high as 5 percent of viewers would click on a banner they saw. Today, the average click-through rate is a meager 0.3 percent.[22] Companies that place banners on other sites would be wise to pay not simply for banner placements or even for click-throughs, but only for sales resulting from click-throughs. Yet those that offer sites for banner ads are not likely to accept this more risky pricing model.

Sponsorship. Many companies draw online attention to their names by *sponsoring* special content on various Web sites—content which is typically related to their products or services. Gatorade, for example, sponsors NFL.com and NBA.com's "Virtual GM: The Postseason" fantasy game.[23] Sponsorship can apply to all or part of a Web site. A site can earn money by inviting sponsors to load new content or sponsor existing content on their site.

Microsites. A *microsite* is "a limited area on the web where the content is managed and paid for by an external advertiser/company."[24] Microsites are particularly relevant for companies selling low-interest products (e.g., insurance) or impulse-buying products (e.g., soft drinks, candy). Take insurance as an example. People rarely visit insurance companies' Web sites. However, an auto insurance company can reach prospective clients by creating microsites on various automobile sites, where people then get both car buying advice and offers for good insurance deals.

Interstitials. *Interstitials* are ads that pop up between changing screens on a Web site. Viewers can see interstitials between the home page and the sports page, the business page, and several other pages on msnbc.com. At blender.com, users can download a "Blenderbrowser" after which they can watch videos and full-screen advertisements in the form of ten-second interstitials.[25] Johnson & Johnson has Tylenol ads pop up on brokers' Web sites whenever the stock market falls by 100 points or more.

An extreme form of interstitial ads is *browser ads*. These ads show up on every Web page by agreement with users, who earn money while surfing in return for being exposed to the browser ads. Alladvantage.com, for example, downloads a view bar to users in which ads are displayed targeted to the users, who earn $0.20 to $1.00 per hour while logged on.

Advertisers are now pressuring Web sites to feature larger ads (such as skyscraper ads) in return for higher fees. But the sites worry that these will upset their audiences. Zeff and Aronson suggest the following:[26]

- Design interstitials that are smaller than a full page because they are less obtrusive.

- Display interstitials when a user's screen would otherwise be idle, such as while software is downloading.

- Make your interstitials interactive rather than static so they are more likely to grab viewers' attention.

Alliances and affiliate programs. When one Internet company works with another one, the two end up "advertising" each other. America Online has formed successful *alliances* with many other companies for creating content and selling goods. Similarly, Amazon.com has entered into an alliance with Yahoo! *Affiliate programs* are alliances that thrive on the Internet. Amazon, for example, has more than 350,000 affiliates that post Amazon banners on their Web sites.[27]

Guerrilla marketing. Companies can capture attention and generate word of mouth through *guerrilla marketing* techniques. For example, Yahoo! launched Yahoo! Denmark by distributing 5,000 apples with Yahoo!'s name on them in Denmark's busiest train station with the accompanying message that in the next hour a trip to New York could be won on the new site. Yahoo! also managed to get the stunt mentioned in Danish newspapers.[28]

Other guerrilla examples include offline sampling of branded merchandise in highly frequented places (e.g., airports, train stations, sports clubs, and schools) and *viral marketing,* offering Internet users incentives to forward promotional e-mails to others.[29]

Push advertisements, or webcasting. Marketers can send content to their targeted audiences over the Web by asking users to register for the kinds of ads they want to receive. Users select specific advertisers and companies, and the marketers send the ads via e-mailed *push advertisements,* or *webcasts.* Before applying push, however, marketers must constantly devise approaches to pull customers to their Web sites so they can get the customers' permission to send the push ads. The advantage to companies is that push advertising is targeted, reaching users who have stated their interest in the product.[30]

Still newer forms of advertising will be developed. Marketers need to work closely with the company's information technology and Web development counterparts to identify the potential and drawbacks of each advertising form.

Marketers need to balance both online and offline advertising to maximize the online traffic. Companies like CNN and MSNBC use their television channels to carry ads for their Web sites. Honda and Armani have won prizes for their full-page ads for Web activities in *Wired* magazine. We now have ad agencies that specialize in helping dot-com companies to integrate their offline and online marketing activities.[31]

MANAGING PRICING

Pricing strategy greatly influences customer and competitive behavior. Marketers always see a tension between pricing strategies designed to optimize current versus long-term profitability. Therefore, marketers must be clear about their business objectives so that they align their pricing objectives with their business strategy. Possible pricing objectives include reducing customer churn, encouraging migration to new technologies, maximizing market penetration in specific customer segments, and pruning unprofitable channels or accounts.

Many marketers believe that the Internet will raise consumer price sensitivity, as it puts buyers only a click away from finding competing vendors and prices. Yet a recent study revealed that the average book buyer compared only 1.2 sites before making a choice, and the average music buyer compared only 1.8 sites. Interestingly, Amazon prices its books at an average of 9 percent higher than the lowest price Internet book vendors, yet Amazon continues to gain market share. Clearly, buyers don't necessarily search for the best price, especially for lower-cost items. Even this may change when comparison sites make it easier to compare prices. Price Watch, for example, shows descriptions and prices for a wide range of computer systems and peripherals and provides links to the online stores that sell them.[32]

On the other hand, a site with unique features or benefits can raise the consumer's willingness to pay. Oracle, for example, provides extensive information about its consulting capabilities, tailored solutions, online support information, and training facilities, with the intention of proving that Oracle is worth its premium price. All of these features highlight the company's unique value proposition and reduce customers' price sensitivity.[33]

The Internet has facilitated more dynamic and real-time pricing, with the growth of auctions, spot markets, bartering, and group purchase power. *Dynamic pricing* poses a challenge to traditional vendor-fixed pricing. Airline and hotel prices can be changed daily, with the aim of filling capacity as the time approaches to "rent" the seat or room. When considering a buyer's bid, the airline uses intelligent software that estimates the probability of filling that seat with a higher fare against the possible revenue loss if it remains unfilled when the plane departs.[34]

Auctions also make prices more dynamic. Online sites enhance the power and efficiency of auctions in two main ways. First, they improve bidders' understanding of the items being sold by providing in-depth information. Second, they expand the number of bidders; today bidders can choose among more than 2,000 electronic marketplaces that auction everything from pigs to used vehicles to cargo to chemicals. The four basic auction types are these:

1. *English auctions,* in which buyers bid against one another, and the item goes to the highest bidder. E-markets are currently dominated by English auctions. Among items auctioned in this way are cattle, used equipment and vehicles, real estate, art, and antiques. Egghead.com and eBay.com are example of English auctions.

2. *Dutch auctions,* in which sellers place their bids and the buyer accepts the one from the lowest bidder. The flower market in Amsterdam works this way as does GE's Trading Process Network.

3. *Sealed-bid auctions,* in which an auctioneer is the only person who can see the one-time bids. For example, a company wishing to build a utility plant would solicit sealed bids so that no bidder would know what the others are bidding.

4. *Double auctions,* in which a large number of buyers and sellers submit prices at which they are willing to buy or sell goods, and software quickly processes and matches the valuations. Stock markets are a good example of a double auction: A large number of buyers and sellers converge, and demand and supply change dynamically.

The advent of the Internet has brought many new possibilities for handling classic marketing activities such as channel design, promotion, and pricing. Companies can now provide considerably more information to their prospects and customers, offer to sell goods directly, and build deeper customer relationships by engaging their partners in dialogues instead of monologues.

QUESTIONS TO PONDER

- How can your company improve its Web site to draw more traffic and business?

- How can your company effectively advertise on the Internet? For example, what role should banners, sponsorships, interstitials, and microsites play?

- How should your company redefine its pricing practices to compete in the digital economy?

EIGHT

Designing the Operational Systems

The final set of basic building blocks—the company's business domain, business partners, internal resource management, and business partner management—enables marketers to design their business architecture platform (see figure 8-1). We now discuss the key factors involved in this design.

THE NEED TO SPEED UP TIME TO MARKET

Companies are eager to accelerate the time it takes to bring new products to the market. A company that launches a product six months earlier than its rivals will triple the lifetime profits of that product. This is especially true in the pharmaceutical industry, where several competitors may be working at the same time on a breakthrough drug. Merck was one of the first companies to figure out how to shorten the Federal Drug Administration's approval time, and it gained considerable profits by arriving on the market first.

FIGURE 8-1   The Operational System Platform

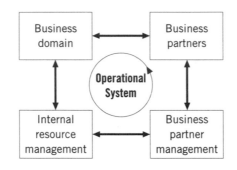

The profit penalty can be severe if a product's introduction is even six months late. Slowness to market erodes consumers' attitudes toward a company and hence company profitability. This reality has frustrated General Motors for years, as GM has watched rival automakers getting credit for innovations that GM initiated. Fast-moving automakers learn of GM's basic research and still manage to beat GM to the market. Consumers form their judgments based on the cars they see, and unfortunately, GM is always perceived to be playing catch-up.[1]

THE NEED TO STREAMLINE THE ORDER-TO-DELIVERY PROCESS

Companies also need to improve their order-to-delivery process. Many companies' value propositions, such as speed, convenience, reliability, and customization, depend on a well-designed delivery process.

The demand for faster service penetrates all sectors of commerce. Weyerhaeuser, for example, is able to command price premiums because it offers a fast, differentiated delivery cycle. Cemex, the Mexican cement producer, made a substantial investment to digitize its delivery process and now is faster than any of its competitors. GE Aircraft Engines set up an integrated logistics solution that decreased its order-to-delivery cycle time by fifteen to thirty days and lowered its cost of issuing a purchase order from $100 to $5.[2]

To minimize order-to-delivery time, a company needs to integrate its selling chain with its supply chain. Dell Computer has virtually integrated its front-end system, where customers place orders, with its back-end assembly, manufacturing, and part and component functions. Customers' orders are simultaneously submitted by Dell to its suppliers via e-mail every two hours. As a result, Dell receives shipments from suppliers every two hours and carries only eight days' worth of inventory.

Incumbents in many industries are making investments to move from atoms to bits. Wal-Mart, for example, spent roughly $300 million to digitize its logistics system. It installed sophisticated communications and stock management systems to provide real-time sales and ordering information. As a result, the retailer again outperformed its competitors.[3]

Customers now penalize companies that cause delays, mistakes, or inconveniences. If companies don't expedite processes, customers will switch to others that do.

TYPES OF OPERATIONAL SYSTEMS

Business architectures will be different for each of the five operational systems ushered in by the Internet.

Click Only

Click-only (or *pure-click*) *firms* are those that establish business on a Web site and have no prior history in the marketplace. Travelocity .com (now the exclusive air, car, and hotel booking engine for Yahoo!)

offers online travel reservations and comprehensive destination and event information. Travelocity.com offers services from more than 440 airlines, covering 95 percent of all airline seats sold; more than 4,200 hotel properties; more than 50 car rental companies; and numerous railroads, tour operators, ferry companies, and cruise lines.[4]

E*TRADE, another pure-click operation, offers such services as automated order placement and execution, along with a suite of products and services that can be personalized, including portfolio tracking, news, and charting applications for self-directed investors.

Homepoint.com is another company that started its online business directly. Instead of competing with furniture stores, Homepoint.com acts as fulfillment and distribution centers for them.[5]

Click Followed by Brick

Some click-only firms find that they have to establish brick operations sooner or later. When it first went into business, Amazon.com sold online books without having any bookstores of its own; instead, it relied on the wholesaler Ingram to deliver the ordered books to buyers. Amazon has now built several warehouses, enabling it to ship books to its customers more quickly. But it still has no retail stores.

Brick Followed by Click

Some existing brick-and-mortar players have added an online site as an alternative or supplementary channel. Charles Schwab, for example, has grown its brokerage business by offering customer services through the Internet, as well as through its call center and branch offices. About 60 percent of the company's current trading takes place on its Web site. Schwab is now the largest single online brokerage company. In spite of being smaller than Merrill Lynch, Schwab's market capitalization is much higher.[6]

In the past, the bank branch was the only channel for distributing most financial service products. At present, however, a number of established banks such as Wells Fargo and Citibank offer online banking services as well.[7]

Brick companies that add click e-commerce typically face channel conflicts. Merrill Lynch resisted adding online stock trading in order to protect its brokers' incomes. But the explosive growth of discount brokers and online trading forced it to enter the online market. A full-service broker would charge a client $400 to trade 500 shares of a $50 stock. In comparison, Charles Schwab charged its clients $30 for the same 500-share trade. In introducing online trading, Merrill Lynch hopes that most of its clients will continue to trade through their brokers. Yet the company needs to provide an online channel for those clients who want to do some trading on their own.[8]

When Sega of America decided to sell its products online, it took a different tack to avoid undercutting its existing retail distribution channels. Online customers pay the same price as store customers, but they are not eligible for discounts and they have to pay for shipping. Sega occasionally offers products not available from retailers as online promotions.[9]

The brick-click channel conflict is significantly lessened when a company owns its own retail channels. Barnes & Noble may have an advantage over Amazon in that its online customers can go to a physical Barnes & Noble store if they want to have one of its products on the day they buy it or if they want to receive a refund for an item on the day they return it. Whether this strategy will create a meaningful competitive advantage remains to be seen.

Office Depot is working to integrate its bricks and clicks into a seamless network to make shopping simple and convenient. OfficeDepot.com provides rich information about its products' features and prices. Buyers can click on products and receive next-day delivery free of charge. They can also check the Web site to find out whether the goods are available for immediate pickup in the closest

Office Depot superstore. Thus, the Web site might actually increase traffic at Office Depot stores.[10]

Brick and Mortar Only

Many businesses fear that actively pursuing Internet sales could alienate their retailers, agents, or brokers. Therefore, they run informational Web sites without offering e-commerce, conduct business as usual, and focus on creating stronger in-store experiences for their customers. The sports retailer REI, for example, has installed a climbing wall for testing climbing equipment and operates a simulated rainfall so that customers can test Gore-Tex jackets. Bass Pro Shops let fishing rod buyers cast their lines into test pools.

Brick Followed by Click Only

Occasionally, a brick operation may add an Internet channel and do it so well that it decides to abandon its brick operation. This happened with Egghead Software. After going on the Internet, it found online sales more profitable and so closed its stores. Recently Egghead software declared bankruptcy and is no longer in business.

THE RELUCTANCE OF BUSINESSES TO GO ONLINE

Traditional businesses tend to move slowly into e-commerce because of channel relationships, sales force resistance, and current asset investments. Some companies, underestimating the competitive power of the newcomers, decide to pursue a wait-and-see strategy. This delayed response is shortsighted, however, as e-business has caught on and industry incumbents have found themselves in an even more disadvantageous position to compete against their e-business counterparts. As Alex Birch and others have pointed out, "You can take part and lose—but if you do not take part, you're already lost."[11]

Such unwillingness to sacrifice the dominant, outdated business design often leads to business failure. Lacking adequate vision and strategic leadership, senior management finds itself totally unprepared to make the virtual leap. As Peter Drucker has pointed out, "It is both cheaper and more profitable to obsolete yourself than it is to let your competitors do it for you."[12]

In today's economy, competitive advantage is more difficult not only to attain but also to sustain. A focus on Internet initiatives is a necessary but not sufficient condition for critical business practices. Because many business concepts are easily replicable, companies must constantly find and act on new opportunities rather than trying to sustain old ones. Companies willing to make these changes rapidly will gain a distinct advantage.

QUESTIONS TO PONDER

- Has your company done enough to speed up its time to market? If not, why? What action steps can you propose?

- How would you streamline your company's order-to-delivery process?

- Should your business add e-commerce and sell online? If the business is currently selling through agents and retailers, how can it retain their allegiance if it decides to sell online?

NINE

Achieving Profits and Growth through Market Renewal

The digital economy provides huge opportunities for achieving both profits and growth. Two challenges are involved: To exploit opportunities, companies need to build and leverage their value propositions and then select appropriate revenue and profit models; and, to sustain profitability, management must constantly renew its organization to keep pace with changing technologies and markets.

CHOOSING A REVENUE AND PROFIT MODEL

A company needs to establish a *revenue and profit model* to cover the cost of operating its Web site or to actually turn a profit. The company's revenue stream may come from several sources, including advertising, sponsorship, alliances, memberships and subscriptions, profiles, transactions, marketing research and information, referrals, and more. We describe several in this chapter.

Advertising Income

Sales of banners and other ads constitute a major source of Web site revenue. In fact, Buy.com gets so much revenue from carrying banner ads that it can sell its products at cost. When the Internet was new, people clicked on about 2 percent of the ads. The click-through rate may still be high on certain sites because viewers may be interested in related sites or products; thus, women visiting iVillage may click on cosmetics banner ads frequently. However, click-through rates on the average have fallen to 0.3 percent, which means that a person passes over 333 banner ads before clicking on one. Accordingly, banner ad prices are falling and Web sites dependent on banner ads will have to find additional sources of revenue. It should be noted that some banners are not paid for but instead are accepted on a barter basis.

Sponsorship Income

Sponsorship is an appropriate marketing tool because many Web sites feature special areas of interest and activities. Companies such as IBM, Sun Microsystems, and Oracle may sponsor content on certain sites to heighten their brand reputations. For example, around 40 percent of the content at iVillage is sponsored. Many companies seek out sponsors because sponsors imbue their sites with new functionality and content at lower costs than if they developed the content themselves.[1]

Alliance Income

A company can invite partners to share costs in setting up a Web site and in turn offer them some advertising of their brand on the site. Alliance partners might want to *co-brand* to lower the steep cost of building brands. A new company can reduce the cost of creating its brand by capitalizing on an established brand name: "Use your Citibank Visa for miles on American Airlines," for example.[2]

Membership and Subscription Income

Membership fees can be charged in a number of ways. They can be fixed subscriptions that provide access to additional services, or they can be charges per use or per service. Disney has been successful abroad with its children's subscription community, Disney's Blast. Autobytel gets its income from selling subscriptions to its service to dealers.[3] Many online newspapers (e.g., the *Wall Street Journal* and the *Financial Times*) require subscriptions for their online services. These companies offer high-quality content in exchange for subscription fees.

Profile Income

A Web site that has accumulated the profiles of a particular target group has an enormous potential for income. Certain companies may be willing to pay a high price for this profile information. For example, if a community had the names, addresses, and other information of 1,000 members who have shown an interest in a new kitchen, and who have no objection to having their names shared, a kitchen company would pay a premium price to obtain those names.[4]

The true value of a community lies in its profiles, whether the company itself sets up the community or only participates as one of many alliance partners.[5] America Online, for example, has built its brand by giving away free hours on the Internet. It attracted more than 16 million subscribers within just a few years. Today, AOL can promise advertisers the largest paid audience of any Internet site.[6] Using the giveaway concept, Netscape built an entire company in less than two years. Netscape's browser had become the de facto standard because it is distributed free on the Internet, while the company makes its money on the server side.[7]

At the same time, it should be noted that the Internet's unwritten code of ethics forbids the uncontrolled sale and misuse of personal information.

Transaction Income

Web sites that feature e-commerce draw a substantial portion of their revenue from marking up the price of the goods or charging commission fees on transactions between other parties. For example, eBay makes its money by putting buyers in touch with sellers and taking a 1.25 to 5 percent commission on transactions.[8] Booksamillion.com makes its money by marking up the price of books.

Market Research and Information Income

Companies can charge for special market information or intelligence. For example, NewsLibrary gives users an opportunity to purchase stories from U.S. newspaper archives after browsing through the first few lines of the stories.[9] LifeQuote compares prices from approximately fifty different life insurance companies. Almost 17 percent of its users become paying customers, as compared with the 1 to 2 percent conversion rate for direct mail. LifeQuote receives a commission of 50 percent of the first year's premium.[10]

Referral Income

Companies can collect revenue by referring customers to others. Edmunds.com gets a finder's fee every time a customer fills out an Autobytel form at the Edmunds Web site.[11] Another example is PeoplePC, which makes money by referring its members to hundreds of merchants that offer discounts to PeoplePC members.[12]

Further Revenue Examples

Within a single business sector, Web competitors often use different revenue models. Compare mySimon and Sony in the consumer electronics marketspace. MySimon's Web site lets consumers select electronic products, search by predefined characteristics, and then compare prices and models. MySimon, however, doesn't sell electronic goods but instead directs consumers to appliance dealers that carry the chosen brands and models. By contrast, Sony's Web site lets consumers do the same thing as mySimon.com but a search brings up comparisons among the features of selected Sony brands and models. In addition, consumers can purchase their products online. These two companies operate differently: mySimon is an "infomediary"; Sony is an "e-tailer."[13]

Early *seeding,* or giving away products and services such as set-top boxes, information, and Internet access, can contribute to creating successful start-ups. The goal is to establish an industry standard as soon as possible and to create a market-entry barrier by locking in customers. Metcalfe's Law works powerfully in favor of aspiring companies with abundant resources. Exploiting this effect will be the key driver in industries that lack a recognized standard, such as Web browsers.[14]

Companies that offer e-mail services for a fee (e.g., Prodigy) have nearly been driven out of the business by companies that provide free e-mail (e.g., Geocities). This is because the potential revenue from advertising exceeds the potential revenue obtained from being a traditional Internet service provider.[15]

Investors evaluate company performance in terms of both the top line and the bottom line. The *market value-to-revenue ratio* is a key indicator of investors' view of the company's position in its industry. Other performance indicators that are watched include revenue per customer, customer profitability, stock price growth, and revenue growth.[16]

NEEDED: ORGANIZATIONAL RENEWAL FOR MARKET RENEWAL

Traditional companies achieved their revenue and profit performance by imposing rules, procedures, and control checks throughout their organizations. Today, businesses place much less emphasis on rules and formal coordination of work. Rather, the focus is on exploring, creating, and delivering value to customers. In many organizations, norms of conduct take precedence over formal rules.

In the digital economy, work is driven more by outputs and outcome than by input. Companies specify the required output rather than the required production method. Given the highly competitive dynamics, market renewal is key. Today, many companies foster in their employees intellectual flexibility, innovation, creative destruction, and results-based orientations. Employer-employee relationships are based on the shared value that both parties co-create. Many companies form ad hoc project teams and use other temporary work arrangements as needed. Furthermore, specification is loose with respect to time and space but tight with respect to commitment and loyalty. Employees' membership in the organization is not defined by their physical proximity (e.g., working in the same departments) or mandatory work hours (say, 8:00 A.M. to 5:00 P.M.). Instead, membership is defined by the deliverables that employees produce and the employees' fit with the company's strategy, values, and culture.

To exploit the digital economy's business opportunities, companies need to renew themselves in one of three ways: by creating a parallel e-business, by building a parallel model in-house, or by reinventing themselves.

The intent of creating a parallel e-business to the company's main business is to maximize creativity and the ability to think about new opportunities in fresh ways. At the same time, though, the parallel business has the potential of cannibalizing the existing business. Prudential, a U.K.-based financial services company, launched Egg in 1998. The online company has a completely independent staff. Its target segment is young, technology-literate customers—not Prudential's traditional customer base. It pursues loss-leading pricing on savings accounts to attract new customers. Because Egg is completely independent, Prudential seems like a venture capitalist rather than a parent company.

In contrast, reinventing the company and infusing e-business throughout the entire organization encourages the sharing of knowledge and skills across all divisions, creating value for all divisions. E-Schwab is a good example. Charles Schwab moved primarily to the online model in 1998 and completely changed its cost structure, weathered the storm of missed earnings, and experienced falling stock prices. This redesign decision required visionary, risk-taking leadership and resulted in a much stronger organization.

Building a parallel model in house is the in-between strategy. For example, the Advanced Development Group within Citibank formed e-Citi in 1998. The core back-office systems have been discarded in favor of packaged solutions. E-Citi has complete independence while being able to leverage Citibank's infrastructure.

Further Thoughts on Integration versus Separation

A company that goes online must decide whether to separate its clicks from its bricks or to integrate its clicks with its bricks. Despite the obvious benefits that integration offers—cross promotion, shared information, purchasing leverage, shared distribution, and the like— many executives now assume that an e-business needs to be set up separately to thrive initially. They believe that the amount of synergy between bricks and clicks is small because the two are completely different businesses that require different sets of competitive advantages. To some extent, physical location and shop layouts are irrelevant, target groups for the two are not necessarily identical, the ability to maximize the width of the Internet product range is important, and different logistic systems are required.[17]

Yet, the strategic option is not either-or. The benefits of integration are too great to abandon. The key to success lies in discovering the optimal degree of integration for the company. By examining which aspects of a business to integrate and which to keep distinct, a company can craft its clicks and bricks strategy to its particular market and competitive condition.

Ranjay Gulati and Jason Garino have examined the degree of integration that makes sense along the dimensions of brand, management, operations, and equity.[18]

- Extending a brand to the Internet increases the credibility of the site but may reduce flexibility. Sharing a brand may lead the company to offer similar products and prices to a similar audience and restrict the company's flexibility to target a different customer segment with different needs or different levels of price consciousness.

- Integrating the management team aligns strategic objectives, areas of synergy, and common knowledge. Keeping separate management teams provides better adaptability to the environment as it fosters an environment of innovation, and such teams focus more sharply on one business model, without mixing it with another.

- Integrating operations can save significant investment costs, contribute to a richer site, and create a competitive advantage over click-only competitors. Separating them allows a company to build new, customized systems and to develop sophisticated Internet-specific distribution capabilities. The decision whether to integrate operations or keep them separate should be based on the strength of a company's existing infrastructure (e.g., distribution and information systems) and its transferability to the Internet.

- Integrating the new e-business allows the parent to capture the entire value of that business. Yet keeping ownership separate can offer greater flexibility in partnering with other companies, provide access to external capital, and help attract and retain talented managers. The key issue is how the company's total equity will be affected.

Companies should try to avoid thinking in either-or terms. Instead, as Gulati and Garino conclude, they should seek to strike the right balance between the freedom, flexibility, and creativity that come with separation and the operating, marketing, and information economies that come from integration.[19]

Further Thoughts on Entrepreneurship versus Intrepreneurship

Companies pass through three marketing stages as they grow and mature. Most companies are started by individuals who live by their wits. Their marketing is *entrepreneurial.* They visualize an opportunity and knock on every door to gain attention. They have few resources to support salespeople, advertising, or market research.

As they achieve success, these companies inevitably move toward more *formulaic* marketing. Their marketers pore over the latest Nielsen numbers, fine-tune dealer relationships, and create advertising messages and promotions. From year to year, their marketing budgets and allocations stay fairly constant. Their bureaucratic culture and command-and-control systems leave them vulnerable to competitors. These companies lack the creativity and passion of the guerrilla marketers in the entrepreneurial stage.

To renew itself, the company needs to move into a third *intrepreneurial* stage, in which the marketers go back into the marketplace. They start "living" with their customers and start visualizing new ways to improve their customers' lives. They need to set their sights on big-picture market opportunities rather than get bogged down in day-to-day problem solving. They need to become kinetic enterprises that are alert, adaptable, and responsive. Their strategy must exhibit dramatic leaps forward in the face of uncertainty.[20]

In the new economy, there will be a constant tension between the formulated side of marketing and the creative side. As Jack Welch once noted, every job should grow to the size of the employee's spirit. Company strategies need to be both deliberate and emergent—deliberate in overall vision and emergent in how the details of the vision unfold.

FedEx is a good example of this mix. FedEx's success is attributed to its "people-service-profit" philosophy. The company hires qualified people and then offers them state-of-the art tools, training, incentives, and career paths to maximize their motivation, value, and performance. FedEx also fosters an entrepreneurial spirit by encouraging its employees to own shares of its stock. FedEx employees are empowered to build relationships with customers, to anticipate their needs, and to take the necessary steps to achieve "100 percent on-time delivery, 100 percent information accuracy and 100 percent instant customer gratification."[21]

Further Thoughts on Functions versus Activity

The industrial age world has been characterized by separateness and specialization. R&D created goods and services, and marketing built brands. Some strong brands are not necessarily the best products, and many of the best products enjoy less success than they might have because of insufficient brand investment. Today, the lines between R&D and marketing are blurring, with R&D increasingly contributing to building the brand.[22]

From the organizational point of view, many companies have begun to realize that marketing and sales are two interconnected activities with the shared goals of creating customer value, retaining customers, and maximizing customer profitability. Marketing staff and salespeople are finding themselves working together under the umbrella of customer relationship management. The integration of marketing and sales makes budgets more transparent and makes it possible to calculate return on investment for budgets, campaigns, and customers.

IN CONCLUSION

The world economy is undergoing a sea change of new technologies, globalization, and hypercompetition. Some people describe this as a transition from an old economy to a new economy. Yet the old economy hasn't vanished nor has the new economy prevailed. The new economy is here, but it is unequally distributed in different companies, industries, and countries.

The old economy is based on the model of manufacturing that came out of the industrial revolution: To succeed, manufacturers must pay close attention to such principles as standardization, replication, scale economies, efficiency, and command-and-control management. The new economy, by contrast, emerges from the information revolution, with its advances in computerization, digitization, and telecommunications. These advances allow companies and individuals to convert "atoms" of text, data, sound, and graphics into streams of zeros and ones (bits) and transmit the bit stream around the world at lightning speed, providing substantial gains in efficiency and accuracy. Businesses can manipulate bit streams to create higher customer value through customization, personalization, speed, and value transparency.

Unfortunately, many people confuse the new economy with the high-flying dot-coms that burst on the scene in the late 1990s. The market capitalizations of start-ups such as Yahoo! were certainly impressive. At one time Yahoo! was capitalized more than Boeing.[23] And when the numerous overfunded, underperforming dot-coms began to collapse in mid-2000, people thought that the new economy was over and the old economy was back.

But the new economy is not only about dot-coms. It is about something more fundamental: the emergence of a network economy. Today, businesses are more able to connect, communicate, and transact with one another and with their end customers. Companies can exchange messages, orders, and payments electronically at great savings. Companies can engage in dialogue with their customers; learn more about each customer; and customize and personalize their offerings, services, and messages. Furthermore, companies can attract customers and suppliers from all over the world; they are no longer limited to their localities.

The message in all of this is that companies must now review and revise many of their basic strategies, channels, policies, procedures, and organizations to take advantage of the opportunities that the network economy presents. New business strategies call for new marketing strategies and practices. We no longer believe that the marketer's job is limited to managing the Four Ps or to determining segmentation, targeting, and positioning. If they are to deliver value, marketers must conduct four activities in the new economy:

1. Identify new market opportunities

2. Evaluate the opportunities and recommend the best ones

3. Formulate the value proposition and market offering that best address the target market's need

4. Propose the value chain that will best deliver the promised value

To succeed, marketers must acquire skills in exploring, creating, and delivering value. They must develop a cognitive understanding of their customers, assemble the core competencies needed in their business, and partner with collaborators that can deliver the other competencies needed for success. With this holistic marketing philosophy, their companies will be able to design and deliver superior market offerings.

To derive the maximum benefits from holistic marketing, companies must digitize their major business functions and processes. Bill Gates claims that Microsoft operates with a digital nervous system.

Microsoft uses very little paper because its employees and business partners around the world can access documents and messages on their computer screens. We estimate that Microsoft's operations are 50 percent digitized. Some other very successful companies—Dell, Cisco, Charles Schwab, and Cemex, for instance—are also highly digitized. Most companies, in contrast, have hardly achieved 10 percent digitization.

Adrian Slywotzky and David Morrison show evidence that the sales and profit performance of highly digitized companies far exceeds that of their competitors.[24] And Oracle, another highly digitized company, claims to have saved $1 billion by using a digital business design. In addition to realizing cost savings, digitized businesses can know each customer more deeply. They develop a learning relationship with each customer through their data gathering and data mining, and so are better able to sense customer needs and recommend other products and product upgrades. Amazon.com recommends other books that might interest the buyer of a particular book. And Dell knows when to e-mail a customer a proposal for an upgraded computer. Dell, in fact, is now seeing each customer as a prosumer, not a consumer.

In this sense, marketing has come a long way from its old economy concept of make and sell. Old economy companies base their business on asset-driven thinking that looks like this:

Assets → Inputs → Offering → Channels → Customers

The automobile industry provides a good example of asset-driven thinking. Having developed the assets and capacity to produce a million cars, an automobile company will try to produce this number and charge marketing with the task of selling this number. The disastrous result is that many cars sit in dealer lots for seventy days. And in order to move them, marketers must resort to costly rebates and incentives. Furthermore, the car company's advertising and promotion cost amounts to about 10 percent of the car's price. Thus consumers have to pay around $2,000 for a $20,000 automobile just to help the manufacturer cover its promotion costs.

Smart companies today reverse the flow of their thinking and plan from a customer-driven starting point:

Customers → Channels → Offering → Inputs → Assets

If automobile companies operated like Dell, no cars would sit for seventy days in dealers' lots, nor would customers have to pay 10 percent more per car to cover promotion costs. And this is the point of the holistic marketing concept: Companies must redesign their businesses from a customer-driven starting point, so that they gather deep knowledge about customers and then have the capacity to offer customized products, services, programs, and messages.

QUESTIONS TO PONDER

- What steps should your company take to incorporate e-business and e-commerce into its operations? Should the e-business be managed within the company? Should it be set up as a separate unit or subsidiary, or as a possible initial public offering or joint venture?

- What are the company's major sources of funds (in terms of revenue and profit stream) and what are its major uses of funds (in terms of operational and capital investment expenditure)? How will the sources and uses of funds be affected if management decides to enter into e-business or accelerate its existing e-business?

- What marketing scorecards should be developed, in addition to financial scorecards, to measure the company's market effectiveness and operational efficiency?

- How can marketers measure the relative importance of the four drivers—market offerings, marketing activities, business architectures, and operational systems—in generating revenue and profit streams?

- How do your company's revenue and profit streams correlate with its share price?

NOTES

CHAPTER ONE

1. Lou Gerstner, from his speech at COMDEX '95, Las Vegas, NV, 13 November 1995. See <http://www.ibm.com/lvg/comdex.phtml>.
2. See <http://www.estorefrontsolutions.com/articles/thenet.asp?section =2.8>.
3. Quoted in G. William Dauphinais, Grady Means, and Colin Price, *Wisdom of the CEO: 29 Global Leaders Tackle Today's Most Pressing Challenges* (New York: John Wiley & Sons, 2000). See <http://www.pwcglobal.com/Extweb/service.nsf/docid/346E77EB01E 8E2DE85256894004F61B5>.
4. Michael J. Mandel, "Commentary: You've Got the New Economy All Wrong, Mr. Gerstner," *BusinessWeek* Online, 27 November 2000. See <http://www.businessweek.com/2000/00_48/b3709097.htm>.
5. Andrew Whinston, Manoj Parameswaran, and Jan Stallaert, "Markets for Everything in the Networked Economy," in *Mastering Information Management,* ed. Donald A. Marchand, Thomas H. Davenport, and Tim Dickson (London: Financial Times Prentice Hall, 2000), 211.
6. See Ward Hanson, *Principles of Internet Marketing* (Cincinnati: South-Western College Publishing, 2000), 190–191.
7. See Don Tapscott, Alex Lowy, and David Ticoll, eds., *Blueprint to the Digital Economy: Creating Wealth in the Era of E-Business* (New York: McGraw-Hill, 1998), 37. See also Stephen P. Bradley and Richard L. Nolan, "Capturing Value in the Network Era," in *Sense & Respond: Capturing Value in the Network Era,* ed. Stephen P. Bradley and Richard L. Nolan (Boston: Harvard Business School Press, 1998), 5.

8. Robert Baldock, *Destination Z: The History of the Future* (New York: John Wiley & Sons, 1999), 15.

9. See Kenichi Ohmae, "The Godzilla Companies of the New Economy," *Strategy and Business* (2000): 130–139. See also Philipp Gerbert, Dirk Schneider, and Alex Birch, *The Age of E-Tail: Conquering the New World of Electronic Shopping* (Oxford: Capstone Publishing, 2001), 47.

10. Kelvin Werbach, "Syndication: The Emerging Model for Business in the Internet Era," *Harvard Business Review* 78, no. 3 (May–June 2000): 84–93.

11. See <http://www.mgt.smsu.edu/mgt487/mgtissue/newstrat/metcalfe .htm>.

12. Quoted in Gerbert, Schneider, and Birch, *The Age of E-Tail,* 131.

13. See Al Ries and Laura Ries, *The 11 Immutable Laws of Internet Branding* (New York: HarperBusiness, 2000).

14. Quoted in Sandra Vandermerwe, *Customer Capitalism: Increasing Returns in New Market Spaces* (London: Nicholas Brealey, 1999), 259.

15. For more details, see Jeremy Rifkin, *The Age of Access* (New York: Jeremy P. Tarcher/Putnam, 2000).

16. Quoted in Vandermerwe, *Customer Capitalism,* 259.

17. Quoted in Don Tapscott, David Ticoll, and Alex Lowy, *Digital Capital: Harnessing the Power of Business Webs* (Boston: Harvard Business School Press, 2000), 7–8.

18. See John J. Sviokla, "Virtual Value and the Birth of Virtual Markets," in *Sense & Respond,* ed. Bradley and Nolan, 236. See also Amir Hartman and John Sifonis, with John Kador, *Net Ready: Strategies for Success in the E-conomy* (New York: McGraw-Hill, 2000), 46.

19. See Martha Rogers and Don Peppers, *The One-to-One Future: Building Relationships One Customer at a Time* (New York: Doubleday, 1993).

20. Ibid., 50–51.

21. Tapscott, Ticoll, and Lowy, *Digital Capital,* 109–110.

22. Ibid.

23. Martin V. Deise, Conrad Nowikow, Patrick King, and Amy Wright, *Executive's Guide to E-Business: From Tactics to Strategy* (New York: John Wiley & Sons, 2000), 141–142.

24. From a private conversation with one of the authors.

25. Lester Wunderman, *Being Direct: Making Advertising Pay* (New York: Random House, 1997), 288.

26. Deise, Nowikow, King, and Wright, *Executive's Guide to E-Business,* 17.

CHAPTER TWO

1. Robert Plant and Leslie P. Willcocks, "Moving to the Net: Leadership Strategies," in *Mastering Information Management,* ed. Donald A. Marchand, Thomas H. Davenport, and Tim Dickson (London: Financial Times Prentice Hall, 2000), 220.

2. See W. Chan Kim and Renée Mauborgne, "Creating New Market Space: A Systematic Approach to Value Innovation Can Help Companies Break Free from the Competitive Pack," *Harvard Business Review* 77, no. 1 (January–February 1999): 83–93.

3. Martin Linstrom and Tim Frank Andersen, *Brand Building on the Internet* (London: Kogan Page, 2000), 49.

4. See Kenichi Ohmae, "The Godzilla Companies of the New Economy," *Strategy and Business* (2000): 137.

5. Paul Timmers, *Electronic Commerce: Strategies and Models for Business-to-Business Trading* (New York: John Wiley & Sons, 2000), 26.

6. Soumitra Dutta, "Lessons from the Internet Leaders," in *Mastering Information Management,* ed. Donald A. Marchand, Thomas H. Davenport, and Tim Dickson (London: Financial Times Prentice Hall, 2000), 319.

7. Steven Wheeler and Evan Hirsh, *Channel Champions* (San Francisco: Jossey-Bass, 1999), 85.

8. N. Venkatraman and John C. Fenderson, "Business Platforms for the 21st Century," in *Mastering Information Management,* ed. Marchand, Davenport, and Dickson, 288.

9. David Bovet and Joseph Martha, *Value Nets: Breaking the Supply Chain to Unlock Hidden Profits* (New York: John Wiley & Sons, 2000), 94–95.

10. Martin V. Deise, Conrad Nowikow, Patrick King, and Amy Wright, *Executive's Guide to E-Business: From Tactics to Strategy* (New York: John Wiley & Sons, 2000), 7.

11. Quoted in Emanuel Rosen, *The Anatomy of Buzz: Creating Word-of-Mouth Marketing* (London: HarperCollins Business, 2000), 6.

12. See Don Tapscott, David Ticoll, and Alex Lowy, *Digital Capital: Harnessing the Power of Business Webs* (Boston: Harvard Business School Press, 2000), 91. See also Don Tapscott, Alex Lowy, and David Ticoll, eds., *Blueprint to the Digital Economy: Creating Wealth in the Era of E-Business* (New York: McGraw-Hill, 1998), 24; and Wheeler and Hirsh, Channel Champions, 190.

13. See John Hagel III and Arthur G. Armstrong, *Net Gain* (Boston: Harvard Business School Press, 1997). See also Philipp Gerbert, Dirk Schneider, and Alex Birch, *The Age of E-Tail: Conquering the New World of Electronic Shopping* (Oxford: Capstone Publishing, 2001), 132.

14. Venkatraman and Fenderson, "Business Platforms for the 21st Century," 286.

15. See Ohmae, "Godzilla Companies of the New Economy."

16. Ibid.

17. Timmers, *Electronic Commerce*, 16.

18. See Dipak Jain, "Managing New Product Development for Strategic Competitive Advantage," in *Kellogg on Marketing*, ed. Dawn Iacobucci (New York: John Wiley & Sons, 2000), 130–148.

19. See Kazuaki Ushikubo, "A Method of Structure Analysis for Developing Product Concepts and Its Applications," *European Research* 14, no. 4 (1986): 174–185. See also Marieke K. de Mooij and Warren Keegan, "Lifestyle Research in Asia," in *Marketing Insights for the Asia Pacific*, ed. Siew Meng Leong, Swee Hoon Ang, and Chin Tiong Tan (Portsmouth, NH: Heinemann, 1996), 87–89.

20. John Hagel III and Marc Singer, "Unbundling the Corporation," *Harvard Business Review* 77, no. 2 (March–April 1999), 133–141; see also Tapscott, Ticoll, and Lowy, *Digital Capital*, 9; and Keyur Patel and Mary Pat McCarthy, *Digital Transformation* (New York: McGraw-Hill, 2000), 18.

21. Hagel and Singer, "Unbundling the Corporation."

22. David C. Edelman and Dieter Heuskel, "When to Deconstruct," in *Breaking Compromises: Opportunities for Action in Consumer Markets from the Boston Consulting Group*, ed. Michael J. Silverstein and George Stalk, Jr. (New York: John Wiley & Sons, 2000), 29–30.

23. Deloitte Touche Tobmatsu International, *The Future of Retail Financial Services: A Global Perspective*, 1995 (internal publication).

24. Deise, Nowikow, King, and Wright, *Executive's Guide to E-Business*, xxiii–xxiv.

25. Ibid., 10.

26. Gerbert, Schneider, and Birch, *The Age of E-Tail*, 129.

27. Bovet and Martha, *Value Nets*, 97.

28. Gerbert, Schneider, and Birch, *The Age of E-Tail*, 129. See also Sandra Vandermerwe, *Customer Capitalism: Increasing Returns in New Market Spaces* (London: Nicholas Brealey, 1999), xiii.

29. Timmers, *Electronic Commerce*, 27–28.

CHAPTER THREE

1. Raymond Yeh, Keri Pearlson, and George Kozmetsky, *Zero Time: Providing Instant Customer Value—Every Time, All the Time!* (New York: John Wiley & Sons, 2000), 45.

2. Joseph Pine II and James H. Gilmore, *The Experience Economy: Work Is Theatre & Every Business a Stage* (Boston: Harvard Business School Press, 1999), 173. See also Sandra Vandermerwe, *Customer Capitalism: Increasing Returns in New Market Spaces* (London: Nicholas Brealey, 1999), 54.

3. Robert Jones, *The Big Idea* (London: HarperCollins Business, 2000), 27.

4. Ibid., 3, 13.

5. Pine and Gilmore, *The Experience Economy,* 94.

6. Ibid., 3.

7. Steven Wheeler and Evan Hirsh, *Channel Champions* (San Francisco: Jossey-Bass, 1999), 195.

8. Robert Baldock, *Destination Z: The History of the Future* (New York: John Wiley & Sons, 1999), 5.

9. Ibid., xviii.

10. Martin V. Deise, Conrad Nowikow, Patrick King, and Amy Wright, *Executive's Guide to E-Business: From Tactics to Strategy* (New York: John Wiley & Sons, 2000), 143.

11. Ibid., xxx–xxxv.

12. David C. Edelman and Saba Malak, "Winning a Segment of One at a Time," in *Breaking Compromises: Opportunities for Action in Consumer Markets from the Boston Consulting Group,* ed. Michael J. Silverstein and George Stalk, Jr. (New York: John Wiley & Sons, 2000), 95.

13. Ibid.

14. Felix Barber, "To Your Health," in *Breaking Compromises,* ed. Silverstein and Stalk, 85.

15. Jones, *The Big Idea,* 37.

16. Quoted in Michael J. Earl, "Every Business Is an Information Business," in *Mastering Information Management,* ed. Donald A. Marchand, Thomas H. Davenport, and Tim Dickson (London: Financial Times Prentice Hall, 2000), 18–19.

17. Pine and Gilmore, *The Experience Economy,* 4. See also Jones, *The Big Idea,* 65.

18. CarPoint provides automotive information, such as news, reviews, dealer invoice information, complete model listings, and a dealer

locator. HomeAdvisor arranges mortgage sales over the Web and offers information useful to potential home buyers, including real estate agent referrals, listings of houses for sale, and a property valuation estimator. See Ravi Kalakota and Marcia Robinson, *e-Business: Roadmap for Success* (Reading, MA: Addison-Wesley, 1999), 1.

19. David Edelman and Dieter Heuskel, "When to Deconstruct," in *Breaking Compromises,* ed. Silverstein and Stalk, 28–29.
20. Kevin Werbach, "Syndication: The Emerging Model for Business in the Internet Era," *Harvard Business Review* 78, no. 3 (May–June 2000): 84–93.
21. Amir Hartman and John Sifonis, with John Kador, *Net Ready: Strategies for Success in the E-conomy* (New York: McGraw-Hill, 2000), 12, 14.
22. Guy Kawasaki, *Rules for Revolutionaries* (New York: HarperBusiness, 1999), 6.
23. World Economic Forum and Booz•Allen & Hamilton, *Creating the Organizational Capacity for Renewal: The Strategic Leadership Program* (2000). See <http://www.boozonline.com> for more information.

CHAPTER FOUR

1. Keyur Patel and Mary Pat McCarthy, *Digital Transformation* (New York: McGraw-Hill, 2000), 2.
2. Rita Gunther McGrath and Ian MacMillan, *The Entrepreneurial Mindset* (Boston: Harvard Business School Press, 2000), 93.
3. See Craig Terrill and Arthur Middlebrooks, *Market Leadership Strategies for Service* (Lincolnwood, IL: NTC Business Books, 1999), 42.
4. Amir Hartman and John Sifonis, with John Kador, *Net Ready: Strategies for Success in the E-conomy* (New York: McGraw-Hill, 2000), 42–43.
5. Ian C. MacMillan and Rita Gunther McGrath, "Discovering New Points of Differentiation," *Harvard Business Review* 75, no. 4 (July–August 1997): 133–145.
6. Philip Kotler, *Kotler on Marketing* (New York: The Free Press, 1999), 40.
7. McGrath and MacMillan, *The Entrepreneurial Mindset,* 94.
8. Mohanbir Sawhney, "Making New Markets," *Business 2.0,* May 1999, 116–121.
9. See W. Chan Kim and Renée Mauborgne, "Creating New Market Space: A Systematic Approach to Value Innovation Can Help Companies

Break Free from the Competitive Pack," *Harvard Business Review* 77, no. 1 (January–February 1999): 83–93.

10. Martin Linstrom and Tim Frank Andersen, *Brand Building on the Internet* (London: Kogan Page, 2000), 44.

11. Vikas Mittal and Mohanbir Sawhney, "Managing Learning to Lock in Consumers," in *Mastering Marketing* (London: Financial Times, 1999), 192.

12. Linstrom and Andersen, *Brand Building on the Internet*, 126.

13. Sandra Vandermerwe, *Customer Capitalism: Increasing Returns in New Market Spaces* (London: Nicholas Brealey, 1999), 7–8.

14. Hartman and Sifonis, *Net Ready*, 62.

15. Ibid., 63.

16. David Bovet and Joseph Martha, *Value Nets: Breaking the Supply Chain to Unlock Hidden Profits* (New York: John Wiley & Sons, 2000), 77–79.

17. Ibid.

18. Ibid.

19. Don Tapscott, David Ticoll, and Alex Lowy, *Digital Capital: Harnessing the Power of Business Webs* (Boston: Harvard Business School Press, 2000), 97.

20. Bovet and Martha, *Value Nets*, 52.

21. Ibid.

22. Mohanbir Sawhney and Philip Kotler, "Marketing in the Age of Information Democracy," in *Kellogg on Marketing*, ed. Dawn Iacobucci (New York: John Wiley & Sons, 2000), 386–408.

23. Ward Hanson, *Principles of Internet Marketing* (Cincinnati, OH: South-Western College Publishing, 2000), 200–201.

24. Joseph Pine II and James H. Gilmore, *The Experience Economy: Work Is Theatre & Every Business a Stage* (Boston: Harvard Business School Press, 1999), 93.

25. See Martha Rogers and Don Peppers, *The One-to-One Future: Building Relationships One Customer at a Time* (New York: Doubleday, 1993). See also Hanson, *Principles of Internet Marketing*, 204–207.

26. See Hanson, *Principles of Internet Marketing*, 207. See also Bovet and Martha, *Value Nets*, 51–52.

27. Hanson, *Principles of Internet Marketing*, 202.

28. Bovet and Martha, *Value Nets*, 95.

29. Paul Timmers, *Electronic Commerce: Strategies and Models for Business-to-Business Trading* (New York: John Wiley & Sons, 2000), 43; and Vandermerwe, *Customer Capitalism*, xiv.

30. Ravi Kalakota and Marcia Robinson, *e-Business: Roadmap for Success* (Reading, MA: Addison-Wesley, 1999), 34.

31. Kelvin Kelly, *New Rules for the New Economy* (New York: Viking, 1998), 15.

32. Patel and McCarthy, *Digital Transformation,* 54.

33. Guy Kawasaki, *Rules for Revolutionaries* (New York: HarperBusiness, 1999), 16.

34. Vandermerwe, *Customer Capitalism,* xiii.

35. Kalakota and Robinson, *e-Business,* 330.

CHAPTER FIVE

1. Keyur Patel and Mary Pat McCarthy, *Digital Transformation* (New York: McGraw-Hill, 2000), 59.

2. Philipp Gerbert, Dirk Schneider, and Alex Birch, *The Age of E-Tail: Conquering the New World of Electronic Shopping* (Oxford: Capstone Publishing, 2001), 79.

3. Ibid., 32–33.

4. Michael J. Cunningham, *B2B: How to Build a Profitable e-Commerce Strategy* (Cambridge, MA: Perseus Publishing, 2001), 9.

5. See John Hagel III and Marc Singer, *Net Worth* (Boston: Harvard Business School Press, 1999).

6. Martin Linstrom and Tim Frank Andersen, *Brand Building on the Internet* (London: Kogan Page, 2000), 279–280.

7. Martin V. Deise, Conrad Nowikow, Patrick King, and Amy Wright, *Executive's Guide to E-Business: From Tactics to Strategy* (New York: John Wiley & Sons, 2000), 114–115.

8. Sirkka L. Jarvenpaa and Stefano Grazioli, "Surfing Among Sharks: How to Gain Trust in Cyberspace," in *Mastering Information Management,* ed. Donald A. Marchand, Thomas H. Davenport, and Tim Dickson (London: Financial Times Prentice Hall, 2000), 198.

9. Ibid.

10. Amir Hartman and John Sifonis, with John Kador, *Net Ready: Strategies for Success in the E-conomy* (New York: McGraw-Hill, 2000), 126–28.

11. Quoted in Ward Hanson, *Principles of Internet Marketing* (Cincinnati, OH: South-Western College Publishing, 2000), 192.

12. Hartman and Sifonis, *Net Ready,* 130.

13. See Steven Kaplan and Mohanbir Sawhney, "E-Hubs: The New B2B Marketplaces," *Harvard Business Review* 78, no. 3 (May–June 2000): 97–103.

14. Quoted in Cunningham, *B2B,* 48–49.

15. Ibid., 12–13. For more information on B2B infomediaries, see Mohanbir Sawhney, "Making New Markets," *Business 2.0,* May 1999.

16. The second distinction in business procurement is how products and services are purchased. Companies can procure supplies either in spot sourcing or in systematic sourcing. In spot sourcing, the goal of the buyer is to fulfill an immediate need at the lowest possible cost. Commodity trading for items such as oil, steel, and energy exemplifies this approach. Buyers and sellers in spot markets are rarely involved in a long-term relationship. In most cases, buyers on the spot market don't know from whom they are buying. By contrast, systematic sourcing involves negotiated contracts with qualified suppliers. Because the contracts are likely to be long term, the buyers and sellers often develop close relationships. See Kaplan and Sawhney, "E-Hubs."

17. Richard Wise and David Morrison, "Beyond the Exchange: The Future of B2B," *Harvard Business Review* 78, no. 6 (November–December 2000): 86–96.

CHAPTER SIX

1. Arthur M. Hughes, *Strategic Database Marketing,* 2d ed. (New York: McGraw-Hill, 2000).

2. Thierry Chassaing, David C. Edelman, and Lynn Segal, "Customer Retention: Beyond Bribes and Golden Handcuffs," in Michael J. Silverstein and George Stalk, Jr., *Breaking Compromises: Opportunities for Action in Consumer Markets from the Boston Consulting Group* (New York: John Wiley & Sons, 2000), 103–104.

3. See W. Chan Kim and Renée Mauborgne, "Creating New Market Space: A Systematic Approach to Value Innovation Can Help Companies Break Free from the Competitive Pack," *Harvard Business Review* 77, no. 1 (January–February 1999): 83–93.

4. Information provided anonymously by a direct marketing company.

5. Ibid., 17–27.

6. Carl Sewell and Paul Brown, *Customers for Life* (New York: Pocket Books, 1990), 162.

7. Cited in Don Peppers and Martha Rogers, *The One to One Future* (New York: Currency, 1993), 37–38.

8. This is a simplified version of the model found in Roland T. Rust, Valarie A. Zeithaml, and Katherine N. Lemon, *Driving Customer Equity: How Customer Lifetime Value Is Reshaping Corporate Strategy* (New York: The Free Press, 2000).

9. Harris Gordon and Steven Roth, "The Need for a Market-Intelligent Enterprise (MIE)," in *Customer Relationship Management,* ed. Stanley A. Brown (New York: John Wiley & Sons, 2000), 26.

10. Ibid., 23, 27.

11. Martin V. Deise, Conrad Nowikow, Patrick King, and Amy Wright, *Executive's Guide to E-Business: From Tactics to Strategy* (New York: John Wiley & Sons, 2000), 17–18.

12. See Philip Kotler, *Kotler on Marketing* (New York: The Free Press, 1999), 15, 29, 116.

13. Stanley Brown, "e-Channel Management," in *Customer Relationship Management,* ed. Stanley A. Brown (New York: John Wiley & Sons, 2000).

14. Ibid.

15. Deise, Nowikow, King, and Wright, *Executive's Guide to E-Business,* 64.

16. Ibid., 64–65.

17. Ibid., 103–110.

18. Don Tapscott, Alex Lowy, and David Ticoll, *Blueprint to the Digital Economy: Creating Wealth in the Era of E-Business* (New York: McGraw-Hill, 1998), 30.

19. Andrew Serwer, "Michael Dell Turns the PC World Inside Out—He's Selling Computers as Fast as He Can Make Them, Putting a Scare," *Fortune,* September 1997. See <http://www.business2.com/articles/mag/0,1640,2679,FF.html>.

20. Deise, Nowikow, King, and Wright, *Executive's Guide to E-Business,* 72–76.

21. Ibid., 73–74.

22. N. Venkatraman and John C. Henderson, "Business Platforms for the 21st Century," in *Mastering Information Management,* ed. Donald A. Marchand, Thomas H. Davenport, and Tim Dickson (London: Financial Times Prentice Hall, 2000), 287.

23. Ravi Kalakota and Marcia Robinson, *e-Business: Roadmap for Success* (Reading, MA: Addison-Wesley, 1999), 90–92.

24. Brian O'Connell, *B2B.com: Cashing-in on the Business-to-Business E-Commerce Bonanza* (Holbrook, MA: Adams Media Corporation, 2000), 175–176.

CHAPTER SEVEN

1. Paul Timmers, *Electronic Commerce: Strategies and Models for Business-to-Business Trading* (New York: John Wiley & Sons, 2000), 15.

2. Harris Gordon and Steven Roth, "The Need for a Market-Intelligent Enterprise (MIE)," in *Customer Relationship Management,* ed. Stanley A. Brown (New York: John Wiley & Sons, 2000), 26.

3. Chuck Martin, *Net Future* (New York: McGraw-Hill, 1999), 33.

4. Ibid.

5. Ibid.

6. Ibid.

7. Ward Hanson, *Principles of Internet Marketing* (Cincinnati, OH: South-Western College Publishing, 2000), 127.

8. Paul Sonderegger with Harley Manning, Randy Souza, Hollie Goldman, John P. Dalton, "Why Most B-To-B Sites Fail," Forrester report, December 1999. See <http://www.forrester.com> for more information.

9. Soumitra Dutta, "Lessons from the Internet Leaders," in *Mastering Information Management,* ed. Donald A. Marchand, Thomas H. Davenport, and Tim Dickson, (London: Financial Times Prentice Hall, 2000), 319.

10. Philipp Gerbert, Dirk Schneider, and Alex Birch, *The Age of E-Tail: Conquering the New World of Electronic Shopping* (Oxford: Capstone Publishing, 2001), 132–133.

11. Robert Jones, *The Big Idea* (London: HarperCollins Business, 2000), 48.

12. Hanson, *Principles of Internet Marketing,* 209–212.

13. Martin Linstrom and Tim Frank Andersen, *Brand Building on the Internet* (London: Kogan Page, 2000), 212.

14. Ibid., 216–217.

15. Raymond T. Yeh, Keri E. Pearlson, and George Kozmetsky, *Zero Time: Providing Instant Customer Value—Every Time, All the Time!* (New York: John Wiley & Sons, 2000), 60.

16. Hanson, *Principles of Internet Marketing*, 308–309.

17. Linstrom and Andersen, *Brand Building on the Internet*, 222–223.

18. Emanuel Rosen, *The Anatomy of Buzz: Creating Word-of-Mouth Marketing* (London: HarperCollins Business, 2000), 42–50.

19. Ibid., 96–97.

20. Ibid., 25–26.

21. Martin V. Deise, Conrad Nowikow, Patrick King, and Amy Wright, *Executive's Guide to E-Business: From Tactics to Strategy* (New York: John Wiley & Sons, 2000), 42. See also Gerbert, Schneider, and Birch, *The Age of E-Tail*, 154.

22. John Gaffney, "The Battle Over Internet Ads," *Business 2.0*, 25 July 2001, <http://www.business2.com/articles/web/0,1653,16546,FF.html>.

23. Linstrom and Andersen, *Brand Building on the Internet*, 251.

24. Ibid., 251.

25. Ibid., 253.

26. Robert Zeff and Brad Aronson, *Advertising on the Internet* (New York: John Wiley & Sons, 1999), 56–57.

27. Linstrom and Andersen, *Brand Building on the Internet*, 253–254.

28. Ibid., 255.

29. Ibid.

30. See Cliff Allen, Deborah Kania, and Beth Yaeckel, *Internet World: Guide to One-to-One Web Marketing* (New York: John Wiley & Sons, 1998), 119. See also Linstrom and Andersen, *Brand Building on the Internet*, 255.

31. Linstrom and Andersen, *Brand Building on the Internet*, 258–259.

32. Hanson, *Principles of Internet Marketing*, 333.

33. Ibid., 331–332.

34. Amir Hartman and John Sifonis, with John Kador, *Net Ready: Strategies for Success in the E-conomy* (New York: McGraw-Hill, 2000), 130–131.

CHAPTER EIGHT

1. Ward Hanson, *Principles of Internet Marketing* (Cincinnati, OH: South-Western College Publishing, 2000), 225.

2. Don Tapscott, Alex Lowy, and David Ticoll, *Blueprint to the Digital Economy: Creating Wealth in the Era of E-Business* (New York: McGraw-Hill, 1998), 228.

3. Steven Wheeler and Evan Hirsh, *Channel Champions* (San Francisco: Jossey-Bass Publishers, 1999), 191.

4. See <http://www.travelocity.com>.

5. Nick Earle and Peter Keen, *From .Com to .Profit* (San Francisco: Jossey-Bass, 2000), 118.

6. Robert Plant and Leslie P. Willcocks, "Moving to the Net: Leadership Strategies," in *Mastering Information Management,* ed. Donald A. Marchand, Thomas H. Davenport, and Tim Dickson (London: Financial Times/Prentice Hall, 2000), 221.

7. Deloitte Touche Tobmatsu International, *The Future of Retail Financial Services: A Global Perspective,* 1995 (internal publication).

8. Peter S. Cohan, *e-Profit* (New York: AMACOM, 2000), 129.

9. Chuck Martin, *Net Future* (New York: McGraw-Hill, 1999), 33.

10. Ranhay Gulati and Jason Garino, "Get the Right Mix of Bricks and Clicks," *Harvard Business Review* 78, no. 3 (May–June 2000): 107–114.

11. Philipp Gerbert, Dirk Schneider, and Alex Birch, *The Age of E-Tail: Conquering the New World of Electronic Shopping* (Oxford: Capstone Publishing, 2001), 53.

12. See <http://www.thesynergyonline.com/infotech.htm>.

CHAPTER NINE

1. Martin Linstrom and Tim Frank Andersen, *Brand Building on the Internet* (London: Kogan Page, 2000), 221.

2. Agnieszka M. Winkler, *Warp Speed Branding: The Impact of Technology on Marketing* (New York: John Wiley & Sons, 1999), 68.

3. John J. Sviokla, "Virtual Value and the Birth of Virtual Markets," in *Sense & Respond: Capturing Value in the Network Era,* ed. Stephen P. Bradley and Richard L. Nolan, (Boston: Harvard Business School Press, 1998), 228.

4. Linstrom and Andersen, *Brand Building on the Internet,* 222.

5. Ibid.

6. Winkler, *Warp Speed Branding,* 56.

7. Ibid.

8. Chuck Martin, *Net Future* (New York: McGraw-Hill, 1999), 133–135.

9. Ibid., 19.

10. Ibid., 132.

11. Sviokla, "Virtual Value and the Birth of Virtual Markets," 228.

12. See <http://www.pcworld.com/news/article/0,aid,44542,00.asp>.

13. Keyur Patel and Mary Pat McCarthy, *Digital Transformation* (New York: McGraw-Hill, 2000), 27.

14. Martin V. Deise, Conrad Nowikow, Patrick King, and Amy Wright, *Executive's Guide to E-Business: From Tactics to Strategy* (New York: John Wiley & Sons, 2000), 148.

15. Amir Hartman and John Sifonis, with John Kador, *Net Ready: Strategies for Success in the E-conomy* (New York: McGraw-Hill, 2000), 57.

16. David Bovet and Joseph Martha, *Value Nets: Breaking the Supply Chain to Unlock Hidden Profits* (New York: John Wiley and Sons, 2000), 255.

17. Philipp Gerbert, Dirk Schneider, and Alex Birch, *The Age of E-Tail: Conquering the New World of Electronic Shopping* (Oxford: Capstone Publishing, 2001), 56.

18. Ranhay Gulati and Jason Garino, "Get the Right Mix of Bricks and Clicks," *Harvard Business Review* 78, no. 3 (May–June 2000): 112–114.

19. Ibid., 114.

20. See Henry Mintzberg, Bruce Ahlstrand, and Joseph Lampel, *Strategy Safari: A Guided Tour Through the Wilds of Strategic Management* (New York: Free Press, 1998). See also Deloitte Touche Tobmatsu International, *The Future of Retail Financial Services: A Global Perspective*, 1995 (internal publication).

21. Raymond Yeh, Keri Pearlson, and George Kozmetsky, *Zero Time: Providing Instant Customer Value—Every Time, All the Time!* (New York: John Wiley & Sons, 2000), 64.

22. Don Tapscott, David Ticoll, and Alex Lowy, *Digital Capital: Harnessing the Power of Business Webs* (Boston: Harvard Business School Press, 2000), 200–201.

23. See <http://www.netmarketingservice.com/MarketAnalysis/MA002-012999.htm>.

24. Adrian Slywotzky and David Morrison, *How Digital Is Your Business? Creating the Company of the Future* (New York: Crown Publishers, 2000).

INDEX

ABOUT THE AUTHORS

PHILIP KOTLER, one of the world's leading authorities on modern marketing, is the S.C. Johnson Distinguished Professor of International Marketing at Northwestern University's famed Kellogg Graduate School of Management. He is the author of twenty books, including the world's most widely used marketing textbook in M.B.A. programs, *Marketing Management.* He has published over one hundred articles and is a consultant to leading companies selling in consumer, business, service, and financial markets.

DIPAK C. JAIN, Dean of the Kellogg School of Management, is the Sandy and Morton Goldman Professor in Entrepreneurial Studies and Marketing. A mathematician and statistician by training, Dr. Jain has written major articles on the marketing and forecasting of high-tech products and on market segmentation and competitive market structure analysis. He has received distinguished teaching awards and is a consultant to many leading companies.

SUVIT MAESINCEE received his Ph.D. in Marketing at the Kellogg School of Management and has worked as a consultant at Booz·Allen & Hamilton. He is now a Professor of Marketing at Sasin Graduate Institute of Business Administration, Chulalongkorn University in Thailand.